Coastal Fishing in the Carolinas

in the Carolinas

From Surf, Pier, and Jetty

Coastal Fishing in the Carolinas

From Surf, Pier, and Jetty

Robert J. Goldstein

John F. Blair, Publisher
Winston-Salem, North Carolina

Second Printing, 1988

Library of Congress Cataloging in Publication Data

Goldstein, Robert J. (Robert Jay), 1937–
    Coastal fishing in the Carolinas.

    Includes index.
    1. Fishing—North Carolina. 2. Fishing—South
Carolina. 3. Fishing—North Carolina—Guide-books.
4. Fishing—South Carolina—Guide-books. 5. Marine
fishes—North Carolina. 6. Marine fishes—South
Carolina.
I. Title.
SH531.G63   1986   799.1'6148   86-99
ISBN 0-89587-050-9 (pbk.)

To my wife and fishing buddy,
Joyce

I SHOULD LIKE to thank the following people for their assistance in helping me put this book together:

Joel Arrington
Claude Bain
Bud Cannon
Ben Doerr
Charles J. Moore
Damon Tatum
and many others

Also by Robert J. Goldstein

OFFSHORE FISHING FROM VIRGINIA TO TEXAS

CONTENTS

FISH CAUGHT FROM STRUCTURES

PREFACE

If you intend to fish the inshore coastal waters of the Carolinas, this book was written just for you. Everything has been included in these pages, beginning with the basics of gear from beach buggies to snap-swivels. The book covers fishing methods from long-distance casting to working a jetty, catching and keeping baits from sand fleas to menhaden, and offers information on what game fish eat, where and when to find them, and how to catch them.

Unlike many guides which are little more than collected stories of personal fishing trips, Bob Goldstein has provided an easily read reference book, chock-full of practical solutions to everyday problems and the kinds of pertinent information which will make you a better coastal Carolina fisherman. Pier, surf, and jetty fishermen will appreciate his detailed approach to selecting, maintaining, and using equipment, how to collect and maintain live baits, and, most importantly, how to fish each type of bait for best results.

One of the joys of fishing in the saltwaters of coastal Carolina is the variety of fishes available throughout the year. The following pages reveal much of the natural history, behavior, feeding habits, and fighting ability of sport fishes of this area. The information on each fish is practical, including seasonal occurrence, abundance, size range, preferred bottom type, structures with which these fish associate, and how they respond to various fishing methods.

The author has chosen to divide his account of each fish species based on the kind of fishing area in which the fish is usually caught, whether it be from pier, beach, or jetty. Certainly any rod, reel, and bait will catch some fish in almost any area. However, sportfishing is different from simply catching fish and includes an appreciation of appropriate tackle, the best possible bait, and an understanding of the fish and its habits in a particular area. This book, based on technical information supplemented with the author's observations and experiences, will provide you with the information you need to match equipment, bait, and skill to the behavior and habits of the saltwater game fish of coastal Carolina.

Excellent sections concerning similar and difficult-to-distinguish species, such as the mackerels, sharks, skates, and rays, are provided with simple keys for the easy identification of individual species. In each chapter, tips are provided on keeping your fish fresh and how to prepare them, with many of the author's favorite recipes from around the world.

No fishing trip can be successful if you don't know where to go. When a fisherman arrives in unfamiliar territory, he usually looks for the most heavily fished locality as the place the local fishermen know to be best. When it comes to where-to-go, such generalities can be worthless. If you want to do better than the next guy in a new area, you need to know the hot spots fished by the best fishermen. This guide tells you explicitly some of the best fishing spots in the Carolinas. The following is an example: "Get on the beach via Ramp 38 and drive south until you come to a barrier of wooden posts blocking further vehicle travel. From here you can see and walk to a very large, broad hole, excellent for big red drum and spotted sea trout (specks) in the fall. Not a typical slough, this is one of the best deep red drum depressions anywhere on Hatteras Island."

Coastal maps of North and South Carolina depict such locations and information is provided on how to get to specific spots. The type of access re-quired, the best time of year, the fish you'll likely find there, and how to get in touch with some of the local experts is all provided.

The Carolinas offer some of the best inshore fishing available anywhere in the world. Here it is still possible to spend the day surf fishing along a deserted beach or drifting along the myriad endless mazes of tidal creeks without seeing another angler. Public beaches and ocean fishing piers occur throughout the area, providing easy access to resident and visitor alike who, footbound without a boat, want to sample world-class inshore fishing.

This valuable reference is your guide to the fascinating Carolina coast. A compilation of facts about the saltwater game fish of the region, local specialized fishing techniques, and the know-how which comes with years of fishing experience are ahead. So sit back and enjoy reading and learning about one of man's greatest pastimes—the pleasure of fishing—in one of the best places in all the world to do it, the coast of the Carolinas.

Charles J. Moore
Supervisor, Recreational Fisheries
South Carolina Wildlife and
*   Marine Resources Department*
Charleston, South Carolina
— May, 1985

INTRODUCTION

The beaches, piers, bridges, and jetties of the Carolinas provide spectacular fishing for many kinds of northern and southern game fish. Where else can anglers fish for Cape Canaveral king mackerel in the summer and Cape Cod bluefish in the winter? Located smack in the middle of the Atlantic coast, the Carolinas border two great migratory basins, the Mid-Atlantic Bight (Cape Cod to Cape Hatteras) and the South Atlantic Bight (Cape Lookout to Cape Canaveral), providing Carolina anglers more kinds of fish and a longer season than anglers living anywhere else. Strictly speaking, oceanographers consider Cape Hatteras to be the dividing point between the Mid-Atlantic Bight and the South Atlantic Bight. The fish see it less rigidly, and that has important consequences for fishermen. The transitional area encompassed by capes Hatteras, Lookout, and Fear is rich in species that in no other place occur together.

Coupled with the rich diversity of species is a coastline cleaner than most, with little industrial development. The great sounds behind the Outer Banks and the lush wetlands of the lower coast provide juvenile fishes and their food sources safety from overharvest and habitat destruction. Except for phosphate mining and agricultural pollution and the effects of heavy metals leached from newly exploited peatlands and excessive runoff in some counties, Carolina estuaries remain relatively unspoiled and productive.

How and where to fish from the shores of the Carolinas is the theme of this book. Because different methods are used from beaches, piers, jetties, and bridges, *Coastal Fishing In the Carolinas* is divided into several sections. "How-to" instructions are offered on fishing methods used from the beach and from bridges, jetties, and piers. "Where-to" information is divided among sections describing the Mid-Atlantic Bight, the Transition Zone, and the South Atlantic Bight.

Coastal Fishing
in the Carolinas

From Surf, Pier, and Jetty

Surf Fishermen in the Fall
(Photo by Margie Rogerson, Dare County Tourist Bureau)

PART I: FISHING FROM THE BEACH

Carolina beaches and inlets range from sandy, windswept dry barrier islands fronting on high-salinity oceanic water to muddy estuaries rich in organic ooze, thick with emergent vegetation and low-salinity-loving fishes and invertebrates. Here and there, outcrops of sandstone or rubble extend from the sandy beach into the sea, while elsewhere the waters immediately off the beach submerge limestone or granite outcrops hidden by dense seaweeds and mussels. Every habitat offers food and shelter to different kinds of shore fishes and provides the surf fisherman opportunities to collect natural bait. Because baits can be used in many ways, the shore fisherman must know what is available, how to catch it, how to keep it, and how to use it.

The principal small game fishes of the Carolina surf are pompano, spot, sea mullet, flounder, and small bluefish. You might also catch sharks, skates, rays, Spanish mackerel, false albacore, gray trout, and spotted sea trout. Methods and baits for these fishes differ, and knowing what works best will make your day a better one.

Some big fish are taken from the beaches of North and South Carolina, and whether they're hooked and landed from shore or from a pier, jetty, or bridge doesn't change the fact that monsters roam our shores just waiting for the right fisherman. The world's record red drum was taken from a North Carolina beach and the world's record tiger shark from a South Carolina pier. Other big surf fish along our shores are chopper bluefish and occasional striped bass, big sharks, big black drum, and giant rays. Whenever I fish the surf, I keep one big bait lying out there on a big rod. You never know what might come along.

EQUIPMENT

Some Carolina beaches are thin strands only a few hundred feet from paved roads, allowing fishermen to drive into parking turnouts, pick up their gear, and walk to the surf. Others may be over a mile from the nearest road, requiring a vehicle to reach them.

BEACH BUGGIES

Beach vehicles, where permitted, allow access to many remote

3

shores. Any four-wheel-drive vehicle can be used as a beach buggy, from small automobiles to big pickup trucks. In the Carolinas, Jeep Wagoneers and Cherokees and Ford, Chevrolet, and Dodge pickup trucks with camper shells are popular. Outfitting a four-wheel-drive beach buggy requires planning.

Tires should be ordinary highway radials, not oversized racing, balloon, or snow tires. On the beach, the tires are deflated to half or two-thirds their normal pressure, providing maximum surface for riding on top of the sand with a soft, wide track that flows into the slopes and depressions. Tires should be reinflated for even short highway driving to avoid excessive wear. If a service station is not close to the ramp between the beach and the road, use a mechanical foot pump or a 12-volt DC pump that plugs into the socket of the car's cigarette lighter. Other essentials include a tire pressure gauge, a shovel, a wide board, a short block of wood, and a jack. Carry a heavy rope, chain, or webbed towing strap.

Equip your beach buggy with an inside rod rack for overnight storage to prevent theft, a roof rack for highway running, and a front rack of polyvinylchloride (PVC) plastic plumbing pipes U-clamped to a board and bolted to the bumper.

A welded metal box frame attached to the front bumper will hold the front rod rack and a cooler, not only releasing internal space, but protecting the interior from coolers with open drain plugs. The box frame is convenient for carrying an oversized drum or shark to a weighing station.

Front and rear remote roof lights are used at dawn and dusk and for night fishing. It is beach courtesy to shut them off when not required.

A board that fits over the tailgate is useful for cutting bait and cleaning fish. Rear PVC fittings are useful to hold rods, surf rigs, and knives. A simple hook and a plastic pail will keep small items out of the sand.

CB radios are fun for bantering with other fishermen and important for getting help. A weather radio can literally be a life-saver.

The care of a beach buggy will determine how long it lasts. Extra undercoating is essential. Lubrication should be frequent, with care taken to treat the hubs. After every trip, the buggy should be run twice through an automatic car wash. At home, the engine area should be thoroughly hosed down. You cannot wash and wax your vehicle too much or too often. Four-wheel drives are particularly susceptible to salt and sand damage because they have more parts than ordinary vehicles. Eventually every buggy gets to the point where further repair work is fruitless. You can delay that day by washing, waxing, and lubricating.

SAND SPIKES

Sand spikes are tubes that, when stuck into the sand, serve to hold rods upright, allowing the angler to fish several rods simultaneously, to work on terminal rigging, and to rebait, all the while protecting the reel from grit. Commercial spikes are constructed of PVC, metal, or a combination of the two and equipped with a separate fold-down spike for sand penetration. But what eases in also eases out, so look for insertion shafts with broad, flat blades. Homemade spikes can be constructed from two-inch-diameter PVC with simple tools. Spikes should be at least thirty inches long, cut at a sharp angle at one end, and smoothed, rounded, or flared at the other end so that you don't cut your hand or hurt your bottom when forcing the spike into the beach. Commercial spikes have a pin through the lower portion to keep the rod butt from hitting the sand or the reel from bouncing on the lip. In a homemade spike, drill a hole and insert a cotter pin. Add a hole near the top for a loop of heavy monofilament; it really helps when you are carrying an armful of equipment.

HIP BOOTS AND CHEST WADERS

Hip boots and chest waders are worn without shoes, but with wool socks over cotton socks. Although the socks tend to slip off your feet during walking, get used to it and don't think it is happening only to you!

Hip boots have limitations, but they are easy to walk in and will keep your feet dry. They provide almost no upper body protection from spray. Some people combine hip boots with all-weather suits that fit snugly around the legs. *Salt Water Sportsman* magazine offers such a suit.

Chest waders are more difficult to walk in but provide upper body protection. Look for waders with leather suspender loops, as metal ones tend to rust. Suspenders must be purchased separately.

Fatalities do occur on the beach, often related to the incorrect use of chest waders. Chest waders all look like they are made for fat people, and there is a good reason for it. There should be room to wear warm, bulky clothing. Do not, however, use the roominess of waders to tuck in all your clothing, which is both incorrect and dangerous. Walking in the surf with open waders invites the ocean to fill 'em up and drag you down. That's how fatalities occur. A single wave can dump a hundred pounds of water inside your waders. Close up the extra space with an outside belt on which to carry your pliers and knife; it is more convenient than trying to find them inside your waders. Even more important, wear a water-repellent jacket *outside and over* your waders. This will shed the water off you, rather than allowing it to funnel inside.

Finally, waders are not made for treading out as far as you can go. If you want to walk into murky water, do it using sneakers and shorts. If you step into a hole in short pants, you can get out; with waders, you might not. Beware of underwater berms during a high tide. You can step through a berm and easily drop a foot or more.

Waders should be stored by hanging them upside down in a cool, dry location. They should never be carried crumpled or folded or allowed to remain in a hot car trunk. For the occasional cut, repair kits are available at tackle shops, or you can use bicycle patches.

RODS AND REELS

CONVENTIONAL SURF RODS

Long casting rods are necessary for barrier island fishing and have their uses elsewhere.

Two types of conventional rods are popular. The traditional soft-tip, fast-taper rod that uses a whiplike snap cast, familiar to anglers from New England to Florida, is designed for casting small lures or sinkers of from one to five ounces. Of the traditional fast-taper rods in wide use, two of the most popular are the Daiwa 910STS and the Lew Childre SU-210.

Long distance conventional casting does not rely on snap casting. Rather, a leader segment equal to 50% of the rod length is rocked in a pendular motion and then thrust in a semilateral cast without ever putting an arc in the rod. Pendular casting requires a very stiff rod. Such rods are known generically as "Hat-

teras heavers" and may be a half-inch thick at the tip-top, ten or twelve feet in length, and very light. Weight reductions are accomplished by using cork tape in place of foam grips, hose clamps in place of reel seats, and a reduction in guides to as few as three. Two popular commercial models are the Magnuflex Hatteras Surfer and the St. Croix 8804XH-10. Using the pendulum method, a skilled caster can throw in excess of the length of a football field, and tournament casters frequently exceed four hundred feet when throwing small, streamlined casting plugs. The method works just as well throwing heavy sinkers and large amounts of bait, although distances achieved will be less. Professional guides on the Outer Banks will lay out a half mullet plus eight to ten ounces of weight for distances greater than most of us had thought possible. The skill is somewhat innate, mostly learned, and developed only with practice.

Building Your Own Conventional Surf Rod

The experienced surf caster soon acquires the urge to own a custom rod. One can be ordered from a rod builder who supplies coastal tackle shops. It is more fun to build one from components. Many mail-order houses and large tackle shops sell blanks, guides, grip tape or foam, winding thread, epoxy cements, and color preservatives and enhancers. Popular conventional blanks include the Fenwick SU-1686 and 1689, fourteen-footers that can be cut down to eleven feet and are suitable for a number 32 tip-top guide. Other good ones are the Lamiglas SB-1207M at ten feet and the longer 1625M. The heaviest and thickest fiberglass blanks are the Lamiglas 1369 and the slightly thinner 1368, both highly regarded by Outer Banks drum fishermen. The best guides are ringed with aluminum oxide, ceramic, or silicon carbide. The typical placement on a heaver-style rod would be the number 32 tip-top, followed by four additional ringed guides extending throughout the outer half of the stick. You can purchase a lightweight reel seat, but many anglers simply place an extra segment of fiberglass blank over the seat position for added strength and thickness and attach the reel with hose clamps.

CONVENTIONAL SURF REELS

Revolving spool reels have evolved dramatically in the past few years from simple ball-bearing drums to precision instruments that use new antibacklash technology based on centrifugal force or on a magnetic field generated during the cast. For experienced anglers not requiring antibacklash assistance, the Penn Squidder remains an industry standard.

For those who want precision casting, Garcia offers a large selection of centrifugal force reels. The model 7000 has sufficient capacity for most beach fishing, but the level-wind should be removed for casting. The larger 10,000CA has a two-speed retrieve and greater line capacity. The Garcia reels use a centrifugal braking system based on four small or medium-sized blocks under the side plate. These can be adjusted or removed according to the developing skill of the angler. The fewer blocks required, the greater the distances possible. The now-discontinued 8,600 has no casting blocks but is a superb reel still in use. The Garcia Striper is almost identical to the 8,600.

The newest distance casting reels are the Daiwa Surfcaster and the Penn Magforce 970, 980, and 990. All use an ultralight magnetic antibacklash system.

All these reels are precision instruments requiring cleaning, lubrication, and protection from sand. New models are constantly being introduced, but check with other anglers before investing. If possible, try some new reels out yourself on the beach.

SURF SPINNING RODS

Many surf spinning rods are available at moderate prices.

However, manufacturing emphasis continues to be placed on good looks rather than on quality construction, and this is particularly true of Far Eastern imports. A few companies provide both quality construction and attractiveness.

An adequate surf spinning rod will be ten to twelve feet long with a moderate to slow taper. Some of today's finer rods are the Garcia Five Star 116H and the smaller SS10M at 11½ (heavy) and 10 (medium) feet. In the same category are the Daiwa Silver Regals 6329H and 6121H. Daiwa also makes graphite surf rods, the PG-21, and the ST910, 911, and 912. Graphite rods are expensive and better suited to long distance tournament casting. Other practical and moderately priced surf rods are the Shakespeare Ugly Stik BWS 1100 and the Hurricane GBSS 102 and 122. A number of excellent models are available under store labels, so do not consider this listing complete.

When shopping for a surf spinning rod, take along a tape measure and a length of heavy twine. Find a rod not less than ten feet long nor more than twelve (unless you're over six feet tall or have arms like an orangutan), compare its overall weight with rods of similar size, mount a reel on it, and determine whether the spacing for your arms feels good. If the rod meets the "good feel" test, then, with the clerk's permission, tie one end of the twine to the tip-top guide and the other end to a low, fixed (not merely heavy) object. Put a strong bend in the rod and evaluate the curvature or taper. The rod should show a gradual and continuous curve through most of its length (slow taper) rather than a sharp curve merely at the tip (fast taper).

There is an exception, of course. You may be the kind of fisherman who prefers throwing artificials, who seldom heaves bait. If that's your goal in a rod, then a particularly good model with a very fast taper is the Fenwick Big Surfstik.

Building Your Own Surf Spinning Rod.

For those who want to construct their own surf spinning sticks, there are many options. A standard, all-around surf spinner was recently described by George Sanderson in a popular magazine. George's preferred blank is the Lamiglas SSB-1362 in either the one- or two-piece option. The eleven-foot-four rod is loaded with lightweight Fuji parts, beginning with the reel seat. The preferred seats are the inexpensive, aluminum-plated FS7SB and the lightweight but expensive graphite and nylon composite FPS 26 or 28. George uses Fuji guides throughout, beginning with a BPHT number 14 tip-top. From there, he adds five more guides at the following distances and in the following sizes: from the tip, nine and a half inches to a number 16, another twelve inches to a number 20, then fourteen and a half inches to a number 30, seventeen inches to a number 40, and finally twenty inches to a big number 50. The reel seat will be somewhat below this guide, its lower edge about two feet from the end of the rod butt. You will have to position it yourself to see what feels best.

There are many options for customized rods, varying with length, speed of the taper, whether one- or two-piece in construction (and with today's glass-to-glass ferrules, that is no longer very important), and their backbone for heaving different payloads.

In the Cape Hatteras area, custom rods often feature gaudy colors, decorative wraps, and thick tip-tops for throwing heavy payloads. The upper three guides are ceramic or aluminum oxide rings, while the lower two are simple big stainless steel rings. Visitors to the area often think the two-type-guide rod is intentionally built for some mysterious purpose, but in fact, the only reason that steel guides are used is that ringed guides aren't available in large sizes.

The average angler can build such a rod from components available at coastal tackle shops or through mail-order houses.

Planning the rod you want and then sticking with that plan will result in the production of a satisfying surf stick, a source of pride for years to come (unless you leave it outside and unattended overnight).

SURF SPINNING REELS

A good reel will have a skirted spool, a minimum capacity of 200 yards of 20-pound-test monofilament line, and ball bearings, and will be cast from lightweight materials. Additional features to look for are a rear drag adjustment, silent or audible drag option, oversized handles, internal trip, and self-centering bail. All reel companies sell extra spools, and that can be very useful. You shouldn't pay extra for alternate right- or left-hand switching of the handle. The number of ball bearings is of no importance, so long as they, rather than bushings, are present. Some of the modern popular reels are the Penn Spinfisher 750SS, Garcia Cardinal 759, Daiwa Black Gold BG90, Shakespeare Sigma Supra 2500-080, Quick Champion 5001, and Shimano Custom 7000. Try out the various options, and don't let advertising determine your selection. Keep in mind that you may not like some of these options.

Spinning Tackle

LINE

Some anglers insist on tournament grade line (high quality control of evenness), while others prefer limpness or fluorescent colors. The major lines are Ande Green IGFA, Berkley Trilene XT, DuPont Stren, Maxima IGFA, and Garcia Royal Bonyl. Many discount stores sell lines at a half to a fourth the price of the premium lines, but don't buy them. These cheap lines often become stiff and brittle very quickly because of their high susceptibility to ultraviolet degradation. Serious anglers buy top-of-the-line monofilament and then replace that line at least once, often twice, a year.

When filling a conventional or spinning reel with monofilament line, be aware that there is more to it than simply winding the line from the package onto the reel. Before loading, lay several layers of buffer material on the spool to absorb monofilament's contraction pressure or "memory." Use a strip of felt or several layers of dacron line. Attach your monofilament, then wind the line onto the reel with minimal twist and under moderate pressure, about as much as when reeling in a heavy rig.

When loading a spinning reel, turn the spool of new line at several angles to the reel to determine that angle at which the line feeds with minimal curls and twists. It may take a dozen turns to show up, but watch carefully in order to load the line onto your reel in the most relaxed state possible for the monofilament. There will be only one best angle.

On conventional reels, there is an additional consideration, and that is cross-loading. Conventional reels are highly susceptible to backlash or overrun. The line, suddenly under great pressure, is wrenched down through the underlying coils until it jams. To avoid this problem, avoid neatness. Do not wind line onto a conventional reel in neat, parallel rows. Instead, use sweeping coils so that the line winds onto the reel in broad, angular advances. Not only will this prevent the line from slipping down through the coils and jamming, but there is an added benefit: it now takes fewer revolutions to throw out an equal amount of line. Put another way, the power of your cast will be translated into the work required to revolve the spool and give up line. The wider your coils, the more line you will throw out using the same energy. It is also important to remember these points on a fishing trip, especially during the excitement of a blitz. During a fight, most anglers pay attention only to whether the line is piling up in the middle, where it might jam under a reel plate crossbar. After a fight, be sure to throw out again simply for the sake of reloading your line in broad, sweeping coils with proper pressure. The spool that has just retrieved a powerful fish is not in the best condition to do it again.

TERMINAL TACKLE

SWIVELS AND OTHER CONNECTORS

The purpose of a swivel is to prevent line twist, and while two swivels afford insurance against one being defective, more than two is simply loading your terminal gear with excess hardware.

Swivels should be of quality construction. Avoid cheap chromed tin products from discount stores, which are made of inferior wire that easily bends and snaps. Brass or steel two-way swivels or snap-swivels are adequate for small game. For large game such as sharks and red drum, use stainless steel, ball-bearing swivels. Sampo makes a nice selection. Avoid duo-lock-type snaps, which slip under pressure. Stay with reliable coast-lock styles, which are easier to use with cold, numb fingers. For terminal bottom rigs, the brass three-way swivel

has never been bettered. Get the wire-ring three-ways, and avoid models made with flat rings, which are more difficult to tie.

Wherever possible, select black or brown terminal tackle, and avoid reflective gold or silver materials, which might attract bluefish bites on a vulnerable part of your rig or, worse, spook the species you are trying to catch. Spanish mackerel usually avoid glaring terminal tackle. Bright materials can be sprayed with flat black enamel paint to eliminate the glare, except for ball-bearing swivels, which are damaged by such treatment.

Nylon fish-finder rigs, such as that manufactured by Jeros Tackle, are popular with surf fishermen. Consisting of a hard tube through which the line passes and a two-way sliding connector that attaches to a sinker, the fish-finder rig is a solution for which there has only recently developed a problem. That problem is the use of anchor sinkers (see below). For ordinary lead weights, fish-finder rigs are seldom necessary and are hard to cast into an onshore wind. The British refer to the use of these rigs as "legering."

SURF SINKERS

When you are fishing a rocky bottom from a jetty or a beach, bank sinkers are preferred because they offer few acute angles to wedge among the rocks. More

12

often the surf angler works a sandy beach or inlet, calling for a good grip in a soft, shifting bottom. The pyramid sinker has been traditional for sandy beaches. Today, new styles are available in coastal tackle shops. The storm sinker has a pyramid upper portion leading to a long, cylindrical, pluglike lower portion. The added length and streamlined shape offer less resistance than standard weights, and the sinker is transported less by longshore currents.

The newer entries in surf sinkers are the English anchors. These are variously shaped weights with heavy, flexible wire molded into them during construction. The wire digs into the sand, extending purchase dramatically. Anchors are able to do the job of sinkers many times their size. Anchor weights are appropriate in combination with fish-finder rigs in a powerful surf with strong currents. They may, however, interfere with hooking a fish by failing to yield.

Another type of sinker is used for working a rig over the sand for flounder. Here, the sinker should slide smoothly, without the jumps and starts associated with sinkers that grip the sand. The ideal sinker is a flat, round weight with a molded ring for attachment to your bottom rig. These coin-shaped sinkers may be found at some coastal tackle shops. A reasonably efficient substitute is the cigar-shaped drail sinker, but drails are expensive and made for trolling from a boat. Drails will dig into the sand if pulled too quickly.

LEADER MATERIALS

The standard leader materials are coated wire used with metal sleeves and a crimping tool, uncoated wire that is twisted, or 40- to 100-pound-test nylon monofilament. Wire leaders are used for shark and bluefish and monofilament leaders for red drum. Berkley, Sevenstrand, and Jeros offer a variety of prepared leaders. Carry a spool each of 20-, 40-, and 60-pound wire, 40-pound monofilament and 80- to 150-pound monofilament for various applications.

For casting heavy artificial lures, you can purchase or make some six-inch long leaders using brown or black wire and black snap-swivels.

Carry a number of crimping sleeves of the correct size for the diameter of your coated wire. If you prefer to use bare wire, you won't need sleeves, but will need a tool to twist knots in the wire. A combination crimping-cutting, short-nose pliers purchased at a hardware store or tackle shop is a standard tackle box item, and should be kept oiled and clean. Get the type that has ceramic cutting edges. Cheap Far Eastern imports are available at discount stores, but they lose their cutting edge quickly and jam after use in salt water.

HOOKS

Surf anglers use a great variety of styles and sizes of hooks for different fish, and these will be indicated under the accounts of the various species. The most popular types are Wright & McGill's Eagle Claw and Mustad's O'Shaughnessy and Beak hooks. Small game hooks are cheap and can be purchased in quantity and discarded (in a trash barrel) when showing signs of wear or after a day's fishing. Larger, more expensive hooks should be selected precisely for the target fish.

An eight-inch file is a useful tool for sharpening large hooks, while small hooks are honed with a stone. Ceramic hook sharpeners are awkward to use and not very efficient. Get into the habit of always sharpening even brand-new hooks before using them.

ACCESSORIES

KNIVES

A long fillet knife should be very flexible, tapering to a sharp point. A separate butcher knife should be used for steaking big fish through the backbone. Don't buy those Tarzan-type hunting knives meant to inspire fear and awe in ten-year-olds. They are utterly useless to a saltwater fisherman, mash rather than cut through fish, and quickly rust or corrode.

For sharpening knives, traditional oilstones are not used much anymore. Diamond-studded tools are high priced. A new tool, selling for about $10, contains crossed ceramic plates behind a hand guard. The blade is drawn across the plates, which strip an outer layer of metal from the knife and leave a fresh edge with as little as three or four strokes. While more costly than sharpening stones, they pay for themselves in work saved and in useless knives restored.

Salt water in a sheath can damage a knife faster than shark skin and make it unrecoverable. Store your knives in dry newspaper or cover the blade only in an oil-dampened rag. Many anglers carry pocket knives for beach use. These are suitable for minor jobs, but sand, fish juices, and sea water do manage to accumulate in all their many nooks and crannies.

NAIL CLIPPER

A simple fold-down nail clipper is handy for cutting nylon leaders. I know a mate who wears one on a string around his neck. Taking up practically no space in a tackle box, it will be one of your most frequently used tools.

SCREWDRIVERS, ETC.

A set of screwdrivers should be included in every tackle box, because the tool that manufacturers include with each new reel invariably won't undo the screws on that reel. Stay away from combination tools into which you can insert a variety of business ends. They tend to fall apart. Get a set of small screwdrivers, preferably with wooden handles. Again, stay away from cheap imports, as the metal tends to fatigue and tear.

GAFFS

A hand gaff seems almost essential to a surf fisherman but in fact gets very little use. Few fish cannot be beached with the waves (red drum, flounder, etc.) or lifted by the tail (bluefish). Nonetheless, a hand gaff can be purchased for just a few dollars, and there is always room in a beach buggy for this small item.

Building Your Own Gaff

If you prefer, you can make your own gaff. Get a one-foot length of surgical rubber tubing, available at tackle shops, drug, or hardware stores, and cut a small hole three inches from one end. Insert the gaff hook into the short end of the tubing and out the hole, so that the short

segment now surrounds the base of the hook. The free, long end of the tubing should be placed over the point of the gaff when the tool is not in use. Be sure the bight of the gaff is at least two and a half inches wide and that the gaff hook is screwed into a wooden handle about a foot long. Be sure your hand gaff has a wrist loop.

A useful substitute for a gaff is a big, barbless hook tied by a short length of rawhide or heavy monofilament to a three-inch wooden dowel. The hook can be slung into a fish in the surf, and then the entire load can be easily dragged by the dowel.

ROD BELT

Every surf fisherman has seen pictures of other surf fishermen with rod belts. Those pictures are usually set up by outdoor photographers with fishermen who caught the fish some time earlier (believe me, because I've learned from some of the best!). In fact, few fishermen bother with rod belts on the beach as they are awkward and uncomfortable, difficult to fit around bulky waders, and seem always to get in the way. On the beach, the minimum is the maximum. If you want one anyway (you hopeless romantic!), buy a rod butt rest. This differs from a rod belt in that it lacks a tube with pin at the base for a gimbal butt, offering instead only a shallow depression against which you can rest the butt of your rod.

SURF CASTING

The vast majority of small game fish taken from the surf are caught by anglers snap-casting small baits short distances with light spinning rods. Many larger fish are taken on heavy spinning outfits capable of handling two to five ounces of terminal tackle. Drum fishermen use payloads of ten ounces or more, which can be delivered long distances only by pendulum casting techniques.

For the beginner, casting with surf spinning gear is the easier method to master. Great distances can be attained with little practice. First, however, you must ensure that the line will not part under the power of the cast, and that means using a shock leader or shocker.

Shock leaders should be at least twice the breaking strength of the fishing line and can be made from that line or added to the line. The length of the shock leader should be at least twice the distance between the reel and the tip-top guide. For casting, it is important that a shock leader supply a few turns around the reel spool, thereby protecting the fishing line during the cast.

Most of us learned casting using the snap-cast technique. For casting lures or light bottom rigs, that technique is usually sufficient. One or two feet of rigging is suspended from the tip-top. The rod is then thrust backward until the rig pulls out in that direction, and then immediately thrust forward, snapping the payload out to sea. It's a fine method for tossing light loads short distances.

Throwing a heavy payload of up to eight ounces of lead and a quarter of a pound of meat, however, requires a different approach. The method has been called the pendulum cast, but perhaps it is more correct to call it the pendulum and the pirouette. It can be easily learned on heavy spinning tackle and then applied to conventional gear.

First, put down your rod. We want to examine a principle before we go any further. Pick up a two- or three-foot segment of line with a sinker hanging from one end. You could simply hurl that sinker-on-a-string from a resting position, but it would not go very far. On the other hand, you could swing it back and forth before throwing. If you hurl the sinker as it is rocking forward, you get a simple lob. Many anglers do the same thing with an underhand cast. As will become clear later, this amateurish casting technique is closer to the British method of long distance casting than our own snap-casting technique. Alternatively,

16

you could rock the sinker backward 180 degrees and then hurl it forward in the opposite direction. That is what you want to do when pendulum casting. It is now time to pick up your rod and try it out.

When you make a pendular rocking motion with your bait, you do so with the aim of getting as much extension as possible between you and the payload. Rock the bait in order to swing it out backward as far as it will go. This is accomplished in two ways. First, you can drop far more than one or two feet of leader from the tip-top. And second (this is where some relearning comes into play), you can extend both your arms out along the plane of the rod, essentially pushing the rod backward. If you had been standing still, without rocking the bait, you could only put out perhaps three feet of line before that bait hit the ground. With rocking, however, you can let out far more line than you thought possible. With this method, you might attain sufficient skill whereby your rod might be pointing slightly downward with the terminal rigging straight out, still in the air barely above the sand, and perhaps sixteen feet or more away from your body (one foot for your body to the rod butt plus ten feet of rod length plus five feet of leader to sinker). The

greater your skill, the more leader you can extend and work with. After the bait has been extended outward the maximum distance and the line has been pulled taut, the rod is swung laterally forward in a wide-ranging arc, for only a side cast can handle all that leader material beyond the rod tip. The goal is to sweep forward and 45 degrees upward and out to sea, all in a smooth, fluid motion from that bait's position straight out behind you.

With spinning or medium weight conventional gear, you will observe a tremendous bend in the rod as it strains to pick up the energy of the inertial movement backward and then release it forward. That's known as "loading the rod" and many anglers try to use it, in conventional snap casting, to add power to the thrust. That puts the angler's attention on the wrong end of the rod and is a habit that needs to be unlearned.

Let's go back to the sinker-on-a-string. The longer your string, the greater the arc with which you can work, and the more speed that can be built into your throw. For this reason, it's important to increase the radial distance (the distance from the fisherman to the bait) in order to have the largest possible arc with which to generate thrust. Now back to the rod.

The cast is set up by extending both arms to the rear and well out from your body to increase radius. If you have a lot of leader out, the rod will be pointing somewhat upward (to keep the bait off the sand) to the rear. As you use the pendular motion of rod, line, and bait to extend your bait straight back and away from you, the rod tip is lowered so that your arms, rod, leader, and bait now point somewhat downward to the rear, the line becomes taut under the pressure of the bait, and you are ready for your forward thrust.

As you now swing around in a rapidly speeding arc to bring the bait forward, pull your arms inward! This very important movement will cause the bait traveling in the arc to speed up, in the same way that a figure skater goes from a slow pirouette to one of eye-blurring speed by simply bringing in her arms and shortening her radial distance. Simultaneously, push downward and backward with your lower hand while continuing to bring the rod forward with your upper. That shortens the radius even more, by transferring the near end of the radial distance, and actually the point of the fulcrum, from your body to the position of your hands.

Stop to consider what you have done. You began with the largest arc possible. Then you shortened that arc at both ends,

first by pulling in your arms, then by eliminating that segment of radial distance between your hands and your body. The arc became tighter while in motion and picked up speed. This is the principle of power casting, and as you will shortly see, it is far easier to read about than to master.

Practice with short segments of leader depending from the tip-top. As you pick up skill, you will be able to use longer and longer segments and to increase your casting distance because of the increasing power you will be able to generate. Remember that the power comes from the size of the original arc and the degree to which you are able to create a smaller arc during the cast. The power is in the physics of motion, rather than in the angler.

In the South African method of tournament casting, the pendular part of the cast is dispensed with completely. The angler simply places an enormous length of leader out on the sand. Then, he moves forward and goes through the entire sequence of pick-up, formation of a moving arc, and reduction of the arc to generate high speed.

In the past, the methods described for conventional casting required that line release be carefully controlled to prevent overruns. Most anglers would use gentle thumb pressure on the inner side plate of the spool to control the speed of spool revolution. That could be assisted by adjusting the spool tension screw in the center of the side plate opposite the star drag adjustment. The correct spool tension would be that tension which allowed a weighted line just barely to drop from an extended rod, neither falling too fast nor failing to fall at all.

With the advent of magnetic and centrifugal reels, all that has changed. For these reels, the spool adjustment screw should be loose, set only tight enough to prevent the spool from shifting perceptibly from left to right. Because the reels have built-in revolution controls, it is important to keep your fingers off the spool during the cast. You must trust the reel to achieve maximum distance.

The distance you attain will depend on the diameter of the casting line, how it is wound onto the spool, payload weight, and skill. You can buy or set up everything but skill, and that will come only with hard work and a great deal of practice.

SURF BAITS

SAND FLEAS

The sand flea or mole crab (*Hippa talpoida*) is the bait of choice for pompano and often for flounder along sandy shores, and for sheepshead, small red drum, and tautog along rock jetties, concrete bridges, and wooden pier pilings. Many a pompano fisherman has hauled in doubles time and again on sand fleas, while other fishermen on either side glumly drowned cut fish or shrimp bait to no avail.

The hardest part of catching sand fleas is finding them. Because they are social, where you find a few you will probably find an entire colony. Colonies often occur near beach borders such as a pier or pile of boulders. When such structures are not present, look for areas where the sand is coarse or mixed with a great deal of shell. Pay attention to when your feet stop squishing and begin crunching. These areas of shell hash or coarse rubble are where sand fleas usually congregate. You may see them scurrying back and forth with the uppermost waves, burying in the grit as the wave recedes from the edge of the berm. Many fishermen run after the individual sand flea, hoping to catch it by sight and by hand before it buries itself. In fact, sand fleas are not at all invisible when buried, if you know what to look for. Rather than hunt individuals, search the beach front for gritty areas where the water ripples back with the receding waves leaving a series of inverted Vs. Those inverted Vs are not bits of rubble causing the water to sweep to either side, but the external gills/feeding apparatus of submerged sand fleas. When you see a great many of these Vs in a broad patch, you have found a colony. If you want only a few, you can dig them out by hand. To catch lots of them, construct a 12" x 12" scoop of half-inch-mesh hardware cloth for running through the surface of the sand. The large mesh allows the passage of baby sand fleas, sand, and bits of shell, leaving you with big baits and very little shell fragment. Surf fishing lore has it that soft-shelled sand fleas are better than hard shells, and roe females (the roe is a bright orange mass tucked beneath the legs) are the best of all. Lore to the contrary, they all work, and you can even put two or three sand fleas on a single hook.

FIDDLER CRABS

The big-clawed male fiddler crabs and their small-clawed mates occur on sandy-muddy-silty shores at inlets and along the beaches of low-salinity sounds, usually among emergent vegetation abutting oyster bars. We have three common species. *Uca pugilator* is light colored and found on sand beaches. *Uca pugnax* and *Uca minax* are dark gray or brown and found in marshes and mud flats. They all can run into their burrows a lot faster than most of us can leap upon them, and the easier way to get them is with a shovel. Also look for fiddlers underneath boards, paper, mats of decaying vegetation, and trash. You can also look for them after dark with a flashlight, while mosquitos are out looking for guys looking for fiddler crabs. Fiddlers are excellent bait for tautog and sheepshead and will also catch a few small red drum and flounder. Remove one claw, insert the hook through the wound, twist, and force it through the border of the top and bottom part of the shell to expose the point and the barb.

KILLIES

Killifish, also called bull minnows, mud minnows, mummichogs, and gudgeons, are the classic bait for flounder. Killies can be collected with a seine, cast net, or minnow trap.

The most important bait species is the mummichog, *Fundulus heteroclitus*, a greenish fish with yellow spangles, white spots, and a white or saffron belly. Mummichogs prefer mud-bottom, low-salinity creeks and tidal ponds inside sounds and are very tolerant of dirty water and crowding. Their hardiness extends to the hook, making mummichogs the bait of choice.

A related killifish, the striped killy, *Fundulus majalis*, is bigger (up to seven inches long), longer bodied, very white, with sharply delineated vertical (females and juveniles) or horizontal (males) black lines and no glistening spangles. It occurs in higher salinity, clearer waters along inlets and ocean beaches, does poorly under crowded conditions, and does not survive well on a hook.

The third common killifish in our area is most unkillifishlike. This short, fat little fish that occurs in low-salinity waters, often along with the mummichog, is the sheepshead minnow, *Cyprinodon variegatus*. A stubby fish about an inch long, the male has a neon blue nape and bright yellow or pink, black-edged fins. Both sexes have broad, vertical blotches on the sides. The sheepshead minnow is hardy and makes good flounder bait but an even better aquarium fish.

ANCHOVIES AND SILVERSIDES

Anchovies (*Anchoa* species) and silversides (*Menidia* species) are both caught with seine or cast net on open shorelines in high- and low-salinity water, but seldom in tidepools or ditches. They are not equal as baits, and that's why it's important to know the difference between them. Silversides are hardy in the bait bucket and will survive for a time on a hook, whereas anchovies (called "hog fry" in the Bahamas) turn over and drop dead if you look at them the wrong way. Silversides require no special care in an aerated bait bucket, but anchovies must be both vigorously aerated and given frequent water changes if a few are to survive. Both can be used as bait for flounder and small red drum. Both are elongate fish, with a silver stripe along the side. Silversides have two dorsal (top) fins and a small mouth at the tip of the head. Anchovies have one dorsal fin and a huge, underslung, basketlike mouth. Use your fingernail to open the mouth, and you will quickly see the difference.

FINGER MULLET

Small mullet (*Mugil cephalus*) are very common along sound and ocean beaches in the fall and are readily caught by cast net or beach seine. Sometimes bigger mullet (up to a foot or more) are caught, but schools of little three- to four-inchers are more common. Live finger mullet are the preferred bait for small red drum, and freshly caught, iced finger mullet are used for big drum. Both live and dead finger mullet can be used for big flounder, and mullet (of all sizes) chunks have many uses as cut bait for a variety of game fish. Big mullet often jump over a seine, but are trapped by cast nets. In addition, you can use a cast net without a partner.

OTHER BAITS

You might catch critters in your seine other than killies, anchovies, silversides, and mullet. Mojarras (*Eucinostomus* and *Gerres*) are small, triangular, high-backed little silvery fish that don't live well in a bucket or on a hook but can be used as flashy dead bait. Tiny whiting (*Menticirrhus*) abound in the surf and should be released to grow up, unless you're really desperate for bait. At about three inches long, they make acceptable flounder bait, but the smaller ones do not. Blue crabs (*Callinectes sapidus*) are protected by law until about five inches from point to point across the shell, but the little ones are among the most abundant food items in the stomachs of surf-inhabiting flounder. You should find other kinds of crabs in your seine that will work as well.

Other baits occur on muddy shorelines, for which a shovel is a perfect tool. You can use it to dislodge a clump of oysters in a muddy sound and use oyster meat for bait. Even better is tough clam meat, and clams can be dug anywhere, with different species occupying different habitats (ocean beach, sound beach, sand, mud, silt, grassy or not, etc.).

A lucky prize in sandy mud is the sandworm (*Nereis virens*). Look for a variety of crabs, isopods, and worms under rocks. No matter what animal you find, no matter how unfamiliar to you, if it's alive, then it probably will make a good bait. Live bait is better than fresh bait and that's better than frozen bait.

While I find it enjoyable to catch my own bait, many other people would rather buy it at a tackle shop. The best baits for catching different fish are described in the accounts of the various species.

FISH CAUGHT FROM THE BEACH

POMPANO

Pompano, *Trachinotus carolinus*, range from Cape Cod to Rio de Janiero and are abundant in the Carolinas. Premier small game fish, pompano appear in the late spring and remain until colder weather drives them offshore and southward. Most of the season they occur in dribs and drabs, but periodically great hordes burst upon the beaches, and the surf fisherman who doesn't drop all else at such times is missing out on some of the best action and eating of the year. You need to know when to fish, what to use, and how to use it.

Pompano are fish of the rising tide. When the water sweeps over the outer bar and the distant white wash settles down to

22

a swell, schools of pompano pour over the bar into the nearshore slough searching for coquinas, crabs, and sand fleas. Any angler can take a few pompano on cut mullet, bloodworms, shrimp, or even artificial lures, but only sand fleas will consistently produce pompano by the bucketful.

Traditional terminal tackle calls for a bottom rig armed with two number 2 or number 4 gold-plated hooks. Pompano are not hardware-shy and can be taken on any kind of hook in any finish. A 1/0 or 2/0 stainless steel, short-shank hook will accommodate two sand fleas instead of one, and that will lead to more strikes. Perhaps the two sand fleas look like they're mating and oblivious of predators.

Short, stiff, bait-casting rods are adequate, but pompano are strong enough to put a bend into a surf spinning rod. If schools are working the surf line, then a one-handed rod is sufficient to place the bait where the fish are, but if they are working the outer bar, then a surf stick is a better choice. Because the fish move about rapidly and range widely, keep several surf rods baited simultaneously and set in sand spikes. There is little danger in losing a pompano from a rod not hand-held. Most of them are lost by jerking the bait from their mouths too soon.

Pompano search the bottom for food, then snatch it up and swim off for crushing and eating. After the bait is crushed, the hook has its best chance to stick the fish somewhere in its gullet. Don't strike too soon, and never strike as though you are trying to imbed the hook in concrete.

Pompano
Taken from Bogue Pier

Let the fish run and pull the rod into a deep bow; then lift firmly so that the fish's momentum sinks the hook. Strong heaves will only tear the hooks away from the fish. Hold the rod tip high, maintain steady pressure (don't stop reeling to "see" if he's still on), and that pompano will shortly come through the waves and up onto the beach.

Typical summer pompano are about one year old, one-half to three-quarters of a pound in weight, and too young to breed. Big pompano, the two- to three-pound, two- to four-year-old fish, remain offshore much of the summer for spawning but appear in the surf early in the spring and again in late summer or early fall. Maximum size for pompano is about two feet long and six pounds in weight.

Reports of giant pompano to the south often refer to permit, *Trachinotus falcatus*, a crab-crushing, channel-prowling cousin of the pompano that seldom travels north of Florida. Permit run from five to fifty pounds, but big ones are not common in our waters. Sometimes schools of young permit invade our shores, but you can easily distinguish them from pompano. The anal (bottom) fin of a pompano is flushed with yellow, while a permit's anal fin is edged in red.

Pompano and permit have fine scales best removed by scraping with the blade of a knife. Gut and ice them promptly, but leave the head on because it supplies a richly flavored oil during cooking.

A classic recipe is pompano in papers. First, cook the fish for eight minutes in a court bouillon vegetable broth as described for croaker. Let it cool slightly, then cut a pocket in the fish along the backbone. Make a big circle of waxed paper or freezer wrap and butter it freely. Lay the fish on the paper. Now, preheat your oven to 450 degrees. While the oven is heating, finely chop some green onions, a small bell pepper, a few mushrooms, and parsley or some other herb. Melt some butter in a skillet, add the chopped vegetables, and sauté the mixture until it is slightly soft. Add a dash of cooking sherry, wait ten seconds, then add just enough court bouillon to make a paste. Stuff the paste in the pocket of the fish. Wrap the fish by closing the paper and crinkling the edges. Place the sealed fish in the oven for five minutes. The paper should expand and brown, and the fish will then be done, but not overcooked.

SPOT AND CROAKER

The most abundant and popular of all Carolina inshore fishes is the spot, *Leiostomus xanthurus*. This diminutive relative of the red drum occurs in vast numbers over the beachfront zone, moving inshore during much of the season and offshore for winter spawning. Averaging a third of a pound during much of the sea-

Spot

Croaker

son, big fall "yellowbellies" may average three-fourths of a pound some years and invade the beach by the coolerful when the big runs are on. A few spot are almost always around.

Spot are readily recognized by the dark smudge just behind the smooth-edged gill cover and the series of almost straight lines on the upper sides. These characteristics distinguish the spot from the almost equally common, but less tasty, Atlantic croaker (*Micropogonias undulatus*), a somewhat larger fish with a pattern of broken or indistinct lines and a gill cover rough enough to cause abrasions to your hands.

The best bait for spot is bloodworm, but some anglers use red wiggler earthworms with excellent results. You can catch spot on other baits, but not nearly as well and sometimes not at all. Croaker, on the other hand, will take anything at all, including cut fish. Both species can be taken on ordinary two-hook bottom rigs armed with number 1 to number 4 hooks. Both are also popular pier fish.

WHITING

Carolina anglers don't distinguish among the three species of whiting (sea mullet) found along our coastline. These sporty little fish are members of the drum family, related to red and black drum, spot, croaker, gray trout, and spotted sea trout. The most common whiting of the three is the heavily banded northern king whiting (*Menticirrhus saxatilis*). The Gulf whiting (*M. littoralis*) has a distinct lateral line, which separates it from the southern whiting (*M. americanus*); both are usually flat gray with only light banding on the body. When Yankee visitors talk about catching kingfish from the surf in New York and New Jersey, they mean our sea mullet (North Carolina) or whiting (South Carolina).

Whiting are summer spawners off the Carolinas, breeding well off the beaches in twenty-five to a hundred feet of water. Throughout their range, the breeding season is very long, and a little different in the Gulf of Mexico. After the eggs hatch, the young find their way back to the beaches, where they occur in great abundance in the spring surf—silvery black tadpolelike wigglers that run up and down with the thinnest high waves feeding on baby sand fleas, worms, and other tiny animals in the surf. Large whiting are most abundant on sandy shores, but they may occur in inlets, in deeper water well off the beaches, or within estuaries. They occur over every kind of bottom, feeding on crabs, shrimp, snails, worms, and clams.

A fish that is one foot long is about one pound in weight, two to three years old, and in its first breeding season. A seventeen-inch fish would weigh about two pounds, and the top weight is probably three and a half pounds.

Whiting are caught in the surf on standard bottom rigs with widely spaced hooks and, preferably, a selection of baits. Hooks from number 2 up to 4/0 are effective. Because the mouth is heavily protected with thick tissue and located beneath the head, few fish are lost from jerking too hard on the rod. However, that's still not a good practice, and steady pressure will produce more landings of all kinds of fish than violent yanking. Many whiting are taken by flounder fishermen using strips of squid for bait, and they will also take a live killifish bait on occasion. Not normally regarded as fish-eaters, they can be taken on cut mullet and will hit sand fleas, bloodworms, shrimp, squid, or any other natural bait fished on the bottom. They will even hit a lure on occasion. Pound for pound, whiting are among our hardest-fighting

Northern King Whiting

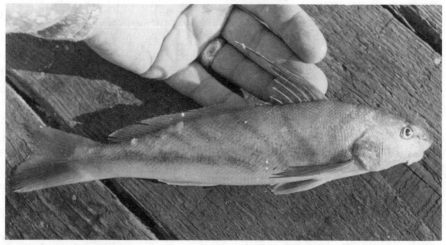

surf fish, and anglers are always surprised when so small a fish provides such a powerful battle.

Not nibblers by any means, they grab a bait and run hard with it, swallowing along the way. A hard strike in the surf often signals whiting entering the slough. They are more active on an incoming tide. Beaches are just as productive as inlets. The top periods are late spring and early fall, but time of day doesn't make any difference. They feed actively after dark, especially on a rising tide. The bigger ones run in small groups rather than in schools, and coolers filled with whiting are uncommon. Instead, look to good whiting action mixed with spots and croaker, especially when big schools of these panfish hit the beaches.

The meat is chunky, white, sweet, and wet, but not oily. Whiting are usually breaded and pan-fried and make nice, large butterfly fillets.

FLOUNDER

The flounders are a large group of flat, bottom-dwelling fishes widely regarded for food and sport, with many smaller relatives that are neither. The Carolinas have four principal species of edible flounders plus several others sometimes seen by anglers. The major species are the summer flounder (*Paralichthys dèntatus*), the southern flounder (*P. lethostigma*), the Gulf flounder (*P. albigutta*), and the less common broad flounder (*P. squamilentis*). Too thin to eat is the windowpane (*Scophthalmus aquosus*). Abundant in our coastal streams is the tiny but very important hogchoker (*Trinectes maculatus*). Later, we will see why hogchokers are so important.

Buried in the sand or mud with only the independently rotating eyes exposed, the flounder is a master of camouflage and subterfuge. It lies in wait for its victims while protecting itself from larger creatures that eat flounders. Catching them requires knowing their habitats and habits, what they will do and what they won't.

Flounders have catholic feeding habits, attacking anything that moves. Their large, heavily-toothed jaws can neatly slice through anything from a mullet to a strip of squid. Their stomachs have yielded small inshore fishes of all kinds, squid, crabs, shrimp, worms, and trash that was probably dancing in the current. Fishermen take them on live baits, cut baits, and artificial lures. My grandfather once ran out of bait and, as a last resort, tied a strip of handkerchief to his hook and proceeded to catch a large "doormat" flounder. Several doormats have been taken in the Carolina surf by anglers throwing large Hopkins lures at marauding bluefish, and there are surf anglers who won't fish for flounder with anything but artificials.

The availability of live bait often determines the fishing method, but many anglers have their own techniques irrespective of what anyone else is doing. If live baits are used, the best are mummichog, killifish, and finger mullet.

For still fishing in the surf, hook the live bait through the meat of the back and toss it into a likely spot. Then settle down to await the series of tugs that indicate a flounder on the line.

If only dead minnows are available, hook them crosswise through the jaws or through the bones just behind the eyes, cast out as far as possible, and then slowly work the bait back to the beach. There are many ways of working a dead bait. In the lift-and-rest technique, raise the bait about a yard and then allow it to drop back and sit quietly for about fifteen seconds before the next lift. For the drag technique, use an extremely slow retrieve, not lifting the bait at all. You can intersperse drags with periods of rest during which the bait sits absolutely still or is lightly twitched.

For both lifting and slow dragging, the strip bait is preferred to the small dead fish. Favorite strip baits are skate wing, mullet, flounder or shark belly, or the elastic belly skin of just about any other kind of fish. White strips are preferred by most fishermen, but flounders will hit dark strips just as readily. What is important is that the bait be fresh and juicy, no more than ten or fifteen minutes old on the hook, and never frozen. Strips should be about three to four inches long, no more than one-half inch in width (narrower is better), and hooked just once through an end. The strip will then flutter (not flap) in the current on the retrieve.

Rigs vary with personal preference. The most common rigs make use of a one- to three-ounce cylindrical or flat-sided weight, a three-foot monofilament leader, and a 3/0 hook all in series. To this may be added an in-leader float to keep the bait off the bottom and away from crabs, or a spinner blade. Both are commonly found in commercial rigs. Anglers who tie their own generally disdain all this excessive hardware and keep their rigs simple. The only important variation is whether you tie the leadered hook above or below the sinker, and again that is a matter of personal choice. Still other anglers believe there is nothing better than a standard two-hook bottom rig.

At times, flounders can be fussy feeders, and several kinds of bait may be tried before you learn what they're hitting. On

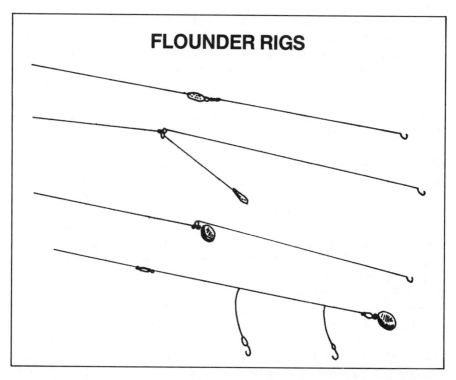

FLOUNDER RIGS

some days they just won't touch a live minnow but will quickly strike a simple chunk of cut mullet. They can be frustratingly unpredictable, disdaining the "best" baits in favor of atypical offerings. At times they will take only small crabs. At still other times you will see them all over the bottom in clear water, and they won't take anything at all.

Flounders are also taken at night by fishermen armed with tridents (gigs) and carrying bright lamps. A coal miner's head-mounted lamp is very effective, but many fishermen use submersible boat lamps and struggle along the beaches with heavy, back-packed boat batteries. Gigging is a southern tradition and on some nights can be very productive. It is most often done inside the estuaries, but on quiet nights the ocean beaches can yield large numbers of flatties. Visibility is everything, and that means no ripples; shallow, clear water; and a strong light.

In recent years, massive kills of young flounder have occurred in Pamlico Sound, North Carolina, and Chesapeake Bay, Virginia. Whether these kills occur elsewhere isn't known, for they have only recently been studied in depth. To understand how these kills occur, you need to know something about the life cycle of the flounder, the life cycle of a leech, and something about that little relative of the flounder, the diminutive hogchoker.

Flounders breed offshore in the winter months. After the eggs hatch, the larvae make their way inshore to low-salinity sounds and estuaries during the late winter and early spring, and here they will remain all through the following season. When the next winter approaches, they do not leave the estuaries with the bigger fish but remain here even during these extremely cold months. They will not leave the estuary until the winter of their second year, when they become old enough to join the offshore breeding population. It is during the winter when they are one year old that several events occur that threaten the fish, so that they may never leave at all.

When the waters get cold in the late fall and early winter, cocoons of leeches that live in the low-salinity sounds hatch out. The baby leeches rapidly scurry about searching for a blood meal from any fish on the bottom at this time of year. Their principal source of food is the abundant little hogchoker. The relationship between the leech and the hogchoker must be an ancient one, because a blood parasite now relies on this relationship in order to carry out its own life cycle, and it doesn't do the leech or the hogchoker any obvious harm. This blood parasite is a protozoan called *Trypanoplasma*, and it is related to the protozoan called *Trypanosoma* that causes African sleeping sickness. However, instead of the parasite being transmitted by the tsetse fly, it is transmitted by a leech called *Calliobdella*.

Calliobdella grows very fast and feeds a great deal during the winter. (It has to, because it cannot survive the warm waters of summer and will die around June. In order that its next generation survive through the summer, it lays its eggs in protective cocoons, and they will hatch when the water is cold enough the next winter.) During its extensive feeding, *Calliobdella* may pick up blood containing *Trypanoplasma* from a hogchoker (or another infected fish) and then bite and infect another hogchoker, thereby spreading the disease. Or, it may bite a flounder.

Flounders don't take kindly to infections with *Trypanoplasma*. The parasite causes considerable drain on the fish, stressing it severely. Under normal circumstances, the flounder is sufficiently active to get food that will take care of its own needs and those of the protozoan parasites in its blood and organs. But during the winter, because the water is so cold, the flounder's

30

Flounder

Fish kills occur when the winter is particularly severe. Under conditions of extreme cold, flounders are too numb to feed at all, but the parasites within them still need their nourishment. The flounders are under severe stress from the cold, the starvation, and the demands of the parasites, as well as the waste products produced by those parasites. This sort of stress may kill just about every yearling flounder in the area. They show up as stiff, somewhat bloated fish littering the shallows of the sounds and bays in massive numbers. Some of them are still alive when found but don't last long. Some of them even show up offshore, apparently fish that attempted to escape but didn't quite make it.

Fortunately, these kills are apparently neither widespread nor frequent, and the range of flounders is so great that fish killed in one estuary will probably be replaced by fish that survive somewhere else, where a kill did not occur. And so you can see why the hogchoker is so important, and how it, the severity of the winter, and the occurrence of a leech all combine to determine natural mortalities of flounder.

Because natural mortalities can vary a lot from year to year, there is no simple way to manage flounder stocks. If there is one thing we can all do to help, it is to release the little

immune system is not fully functional. Although the flounder can make protective antibodies to something it became immune to during the warm season just past, it cannot initiate any new immunities when the water is this cold. And the blood parasite is new. If the flounder can just hang on until the water warms in the spring, it can initiate a new immune response and get rid of those nasty blood parasites. For now, however, all it can do is feed to the best of its ability in an effort to provide food for itself and its parasites.

31

ones. The minimum size for taking flounder in North Carolina is eleven inches total length, but there is no minimum length in South Carolina. You cannot have large flounders if you won't release the small ones, and biologists have shown that you can land more pounds of them if you let the little ones grow up, even with natural mortality along the way.

Most anglers fillet flounder, cutting four strips per fish for breading and deep-frying. The bones and head juices of flounder contribute to the rich flavor, and if you are willing to put up with the bones, you will be rewarded for your efforts. A good method is to deep fry them whole and serve them with a flood of melted butter laced with fresh parsley. In Carolina restaurants, flounder stuffed with crabmeat is very popular, the crab inserted into a pocket cut into the skin of the fish. Flounders may also be planked outdoors or grilled with a slice of bacon. Alternatively, try steaming the fish over water in a covered pot after coating it thoroughly with soy sauce, scraped ginger root, sliced green onions, and Chinese salted soybeans.

SNAPPER BLUEFISH

Bluefish (*Pomatomus saltatrix*) come in all sizes, from the four-ounce "snappers" that cavort through our sounds and along the summer beaches to the monster spring and fall "choppers" that overwinter off the Carolina capes. For both the experienced angler and the young novice with a light freshwater outfit, catching small bluefish is often the best fun of the day.

While many fishermen might disagree regarding the culinary excellence of choppers, few complain about the sweetness of a snapper. And little blues are not only good to eat; king mackerel fishermen regard snapper blues as premier live baits.

Small blues can be caught on any bait at all, but for great sport you cannot beat taking them on rapidly retrieved artificial lures. Some of the favorite beach lures for small blues are the Hopkins No = EQL with or without a bucktail on a single or treble hook, the Hopkins 7S, the Krokodile Spoon, and the Conner Z1H. All are available at coastal tackle shops. The inland fisherman coming to visit the coast should rummage through the old tackle box for a heavy Dardevle spoon, either freshly painted with a bold red stripe or polished to a gleaming silver. Blues will hit anything shiny or red. You can also use sinking plugs like the Gotcha and Jerk Jigger. The white body and red head models are most effective. All these lures have great weight for their size and cast well. But since they're not cheap, you don't want to lose them.

Bluefish have razor-sharp teeth capable of cutting monofilament lines. Wire leaders are essential in avoiding cutoffs and lost lures. Whether or not a shock leader terminates the fishing line, the business end of your rig should begin with a small black swivel. From the swivel, tie a short length, perhaps six inches, of black wire, and end the rig with a black snap or snap-swivel that enables you to switch lures quickly. The flat black finish is important; otherwise blues are likely to attack your hardware instead of your lure, resulting in cutoffs.

Small blues are usually within casting range of a light spinning outfit loaded with six- to ten-pound-test line. At times large schools of two- to three-pound "tailors" move inshore, usually marked by diving birds feeding on baitfish. It may be necessary to cast greater distances, in which case big rods and twelve- to fifteen-pound-test line are appropriate.

DOGFISH, SKATES, AND RAYS

In common with the sharks, all the dogfish, skates, and rays have skeletons made entirely of cartilage, which classifies them as elasmobranchs, a natural group of animals as different from fishes with bony skeletons (teleosts) as frogs and sala-

manders (amphibians) are from snakes and lizards (reptiles). Of the many kinds found on the Carolina coast, a few are abundant. In winter, the most common small beach shark is the spiny dogfish (*Squalus acanthius*). The rest of the year, smooth dogfish (*Mustelus canis*) take their place. (The horny spines in front of the dorsal fins distinguish the spiny from the smooth dogfish.) The sandpaperlike teeth of dogfish separate them from small requiem sharks (*Carcharhinus*), which have very sharklike triangular teeth capable of cutting a careless angler rather seriously.

The spiny dogfish used to be a valuable fish in fish-and-chips, but today flounders are more often used. All small sharks are quite tasty if prepared properly. They should be immediately gutted and the tail removed to bleed them out thoroughly, then buried in ice. Before cooking, they should be cut into small pieces or deeply gouged with a blade, and then soaked in a citrus bath for a few hours. I use the juice of two whole lemons to a quart of water, but you can use grapefruit juice or even plain vinegar. The same instructions apply to skates and rays.

Of the many kinds of skates on the Carolina coast, our most common is the clearnosed skate (*Raja eglanteria*). Skates don't have stingers, but they can bite very hard with their sandpaper jaws, and their tails can abrade an ungloved hand with many tiny, irritating spines. Skates are migratory, but the males and females make separate migrations. In males, the pelvic fins surrounding the vent are modified into very unfishlike "claspers," but these fins are unmodified and quite fishlike in females. Since this is true of all the elasmobranch fishes, you now know how to tell the sex of sharks, skates, rays, and sawfishes. Skates lay eggs in geometric, brown egg cases ("mermaid's purses"), which you have seen washed up on the beach.

Several types of rays frequent our coast, and all of them have stingers except for the rare smooth butterfly ray (*Gymnura micrura*); its larger relative, the spiny butterfly ray (*G. altavela*), is well armed. Butterfly rays are much wider than long. A large, brown ray without markings but with a mantalike indented head is the cownose ray (*Rhinoptera bonasus*), while another large brown ray with white polka dots and a protruding snout is the spotted eagle ray (*Aetobatus narinari*). The uncommon bullnose ray (*Myliobatis freminvillei*) also has a protruding snout, but lacks polka dots. None of these rays is common on the beach. The common beach rays are the stingrays (*Dasyatis sabina*, *D. americana*, and *D. sayi*). These rays are brownish-black with whiplike tails. The stingers of all rays are at the base, not the tip, so don't worry about being stung by a thrashing tail.

If you do not intend to use a skate or ray, pick it up and throw it back without mutilation. To pick up a ray or skate safely, position yourself directly in front. Reach down and insert your fingers into the spiracles behind the eyes. With the fish now pointing its tail and stinger(s) away from you, it can be handled in perfect safety.

Although rays and skates are edible, they are seldom taken for this purpose. The Virginia Institute of Marine Sciences (VIMS) is attempting to popularize the cownose ray as a food fish, but their efforts are not starting any fires among domestic fishermen. Ray and skate wings make good flounder strip bait. Whole or halved rays and skates are excellent baits for big sharks.

SPANISH MACKEREL

Spanish mackerel (*Scomberomorus maculatus*) dash up and down the high-salinity ocean beaches in the summer, even entering inlets on a flooding tide. Sometimes they are mixed with small bluefish, but more often they occur in separate schools. Most are caught from boats or piers, but some are taken from shore. They can be caught with small, silvery lures tied directly to a heavy monofilament leader, with no swivels, snaps, or other hardware anywhere on the rig. Favorite lures are the Hopkins Shorty, Hopkins No = EQL, Acme Kastmaster, and Conner Z1H.

LITTLE TUNNY

Little tunny, false albacore or "Fat Alberts" (*Euthynnus alletteratus*), hit the beaches during the spring and fall, always accompanied by small groups of diving terns. Up close, you can see the fish crashing through the surface after silversides and anchovies, their principal forage fish. For little tunny, you must cast far and retrieve at very high speed, placing the small, silvery lure right where the fish is expected to be at the time the lure hits the water. A light spinning outfit loaded with eight- to ten-pound-test monofilament line will do the job. Use a heavy monofilament shock leader but no hardware. The lure must be small and heavy for long casts. Favorites are the Sting Silver and the Conner Z1H. Little tunny are powerful fish, averaging four to eight pounds in weight, and all of it dynamite. Little tunny are frequently caught from piers. They also occur with big chopper bluefish.

SPOTTED SEA TROUT

Spotted sea trout or speckled trout (*Cynoscion nebulosus*) spend much of the time in inlets and sound channels but come out to the ocean beaches in winter. In fact, Palmetto State anglers call them "winter trout." Their occurrence is not very predictable,

Spanish Mackerel

but when you find them, Miro-Lures are very effective. Get a selection of colors, because specks are fussy. Other good artificials are Mann's Sting Ray Grubs in the large firetail (WFT4) and green (G4) models, Bett's Spec Rig, and the Sting Silver. Keep a variety of lures on hand. Specks are also taken on live shrimp, pinfish, or spot suspended from a float.

If you think this selection means that specks can be taken on just about anything, think again. The selection indicates what they might hit at any one time. The strange and even unique behavior of specks is that they usually hit one item and won't touch anything else.

Heavy monofilament leaders will generate more hits than wire. The minimum legal size in South Carolina is twelve inches.

GRAY SEA TROUT

Related to specks is the gray sea trout, summer trout, or weakfish (*Cynoscion regalis*). Gray trout may be taken in the surf at any time of the year but more often during spring and fall. They will hit squid strips fished for flounder, or cut mullet lying on the bottom. Gray trout can be taken on various lures in the surf, including Hopkins spoons (all sizes), Firetail Sting Ray

14 lb. 14 oz. Weakfish
North Carolina State Record – Caught by Sterling Ammons at Coquina Beach Nags Head (Photo by Dare County Tourist Bureau)

Grubs, Mister Twisters, Bett's Sand Bass Rig, Jerk Jiggers, Gotchas, and Sting Silvers. Stay away from red finishes to avoid bluefish. In Sting Silvers and related lures, use light green or silver. In Jerk Jiggers and Gotchas, use blue heads on white bodies and, for added effectiveness, tie on a twelve-inch monofilament dropper carrying a streamer fly behind the lure. Big gray trout can also be taken on big live baits.

RED DRUM

The red drum (*Sciaenops ocellata*) has many names even within the Carolinas, including channel bass, spottail bass, redfish, and puppy drum (for the little ones). From the Delmarva Peninsula to the Gulf Coast, separate populations of red drum occupy the different sounds and estuaries, coming out of the deeper inlets in the fall to spawn in ocean waters near cuts between barrier islands. The adult fish will conclude the spawning season in late fall by migrating to their offshore wintering grounds. They will return to the beaches and inlets in the spring.

Red drum move inside for the warm season, feeding in the sounds and estuaries, sometimes moving into almost fresh waters up toward the head of the estuary. Commercial fishermen take numbers of them in nets fixed near river deltas. This tolerance for water of extremely low salinity, so long as it has plenty of dissolved mineral hardness, has enabled the Texas Parks and Wildlife Department to stock red drum (and recently, red-black drum hybrids) in inland hardwater lakes.

The fall-spawned red drum larvae leave the nearshore ocean waters and move into the protected sounds and estuaries for their first winter. Here they grow rapidly and remain until old enough to join their larger relatives. Many of these young fish won't survive predation, harvest by netters, pollution, or just bad weather. All data indicate a good year class was produced in 1981, and that group of fish should provide excellent fishing at least into the 1990s.

Big red drum may be twenty years old or more, and they don't get any bigger than the giants that live in North Carolina's Pamlico Sound. These fish are monsters compared with their southern cousins, and they have provided just about all the record fish in all line classes over the years. The current world record is a 94-pounder taken at Hatteras Island on November 7, 1984, beating out a 90-pounder taken eleven years to the day previously on the same island. The big reds taken from the beaches of Virginia are believed to be migrants from Pamlico Sound rather than a local popu-

37

lation. There appears to be another population of large red drum in Fripp Inlet, South Carolina, but where they go is a mystery. Smaller red drum can be taken just about everywhere in our region.

Fishing for big red drum is a specialty of the Outer Banks inlets, sounds, and beaches. Big surf sticks are used for big drum, in part because a strong rod is necessary to throw a great deal of bait a long distance, and in part because a heavy stick can put pressure on one of these copper-colored trophies. Standard tackle is a conventional or spinning rod loaded with 17- to 25-pound-test monofilament line and a long shock leader of either doubled line or a segment of 40- to 60-pound-test single line. Two methods of terminal rigging are popular on the beaches, and even the guides agree that it probably doesn't make a great deal of difference to the fish which rig you use.

The standard fixed bottom rig consists of a three-way brass wire swivel tied to the shock leader, to a sinker through a short dropper or clip, and to a snelled hook. Storm sinkers are popular on the beach for big drum, but some anglers use an anchor weight if nothing else will hold bottom. The hook is a short-shanked 8/0 or 9/0 claw hook with a recurved eye to better hold the snell. Most anglers use about six to ten inches of leader material consisting of 80- to 150-pound-test limp monofilament, depending on their tying skills. A three-way fixed bottom rig is the preferred terminal tackle when casting into a head wind with a big bait.

The other standard bottom rig is the slider, leger, or fish-finder rig. The shock leader will be tied to a sinker through a swivel and sliding clip or facsimile. A snelled hook is used, with about six to ten inches of 80- to 150-pound-test monofilament hook leader material ending at a black barrel swivel; the snelled hooks should be made up in advance. To rig up on the beach, the fishing line is doubled or 40- to 60-pound monofilament added to create the shock leader. Then, the swivel of the snelled hook is slid onto the shock leader, and the shock leader sealed off by adding the storm or anchor sinker. This rig works well when you are casting with the wind at your back. (If you try to throw it into an onshore wind, the wind will blow the bait back up the shocker toward you during the cast.)

If big bluefish are around, use either the heaviest monofilament leader (150-pound-test) or black wire. Coated multistrand wire can be twisted and the coating melted with a flame, or it can be crimped, while single-strand uncoated wire can be twisted to

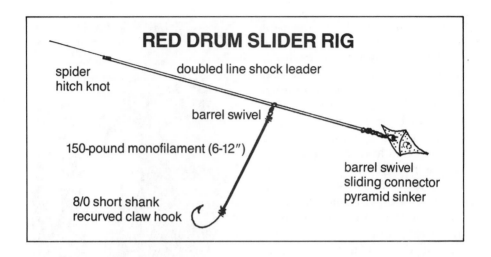

RED DRUM SLIDER RIG

spider
hitch knot

doubled line shock leader

barrel swivel

150-pound monofilament (6-12″)

barrel swivel
sliding connector
pyramid sinker

8/0 short shank
recurved claw hook

form a tight knot. Anchor sinkers provide an excellent grip in a strong current but also may interfere with striking a fish on the pickup. They are not popular for big drum.

Baits are a matter of personal preference, and every guide and expert swears by something else. The most popular baits (and they all work) are mullet (heads, fillets, chunks, or whole finger-sized fish), chunks of menhaden, shad, or herring, the head of a spot or croaker, or a fillet of bluefish. People also catch red drum on crab-clam sandwiches, as used for red and black drum in Virginia. The key is to have a big, fresh (never frozen) bait that is still leaking juices. Keep a fresh bait out there no longer than fifteen minutes, and attend to your rod. Crabs, dogfish sharks, and small bluefish will chew your bait, so change it fre-

quently. Bare hooks or drained-out baits don't catch drum.

Watch your line at all times. Don't close your eyes and rely on hearing the ratchet buzz. Novices may quit after dark or wander down the beach for a social conversation. Bad habits lose fish. A drum will often as not pick up a bait and swim toward the beach. You won't hear the ratchet and your rod won't bend. Instead, the line will rapidly go slack. If you see it happen, reel in the slack and hit the fish hard.

Red drum can be caught around the clock. There is no best time of day or night, and no best tide. What you want is a lot of bait in the water, a turbulent surf that will bring the fish in close to the beach, and a good location for the time of year. Best times on the beaches are April and November. There are hot spots, which will be covered later in the book.

There are two ways to hook drum. Many anglers let the fish run a long time before they take in slack, lean back, and set the hook hard. In the meantime, a lot of drum will chew the juices from the bait and drop it, changing their minds about that particular meal. Most regulars sting the fish almost immediately to solve both the problem of drops and the problem of releasing them alive. A drum allowed to run may swallow the bait and be gut-hooked, and that fish may not survive release. The regulars catch plenty of them, and they don't like to chance killing one of these magnificent fish. They sting the fish right away, trying for a lip or jaw hookup, and would rather miss the fish than kill it. This is another reason why you should always sharpen your hooks, especially new hooks, before laying a bait out there in the slough.

Red drum are fighters that will provide plenty of action for the most demanding sportsman. They don't jump, and their runs are not spectacular reel-strippers. But the fish are very strong and provide an agonizingly heavy fight. You will have lots of sport with even heavy tackle, so don't feel the need to make your gear more sporty and less reliable. Watch the regulars; you won't see very many of them using light tackle.

94 lb. 2 oz. Red Drum
IGFA World Record – Caught by David Deuel near Avon, North Carolina (Photo by Margie Rogerson, Dare County Tourist Bureau)

Red drum can be beached by using the lift of the waves. If the fish is well hooked, you can ease it up on the beach by grabbing the terminal tackle. Some anglers use a portable gaff hook or a hand gaff and stick the fish in a lip or the lower jaw so that it may be released with minimal damage.

The best locations for big red drum are the points of capes, the deeper channels of inlets, along jetties, and at rips that wash out through the breaks between offshore bars. Look for interruptions in the white water well off the beach, for that is where the inner slough water is rushing back outside and where the fish are likely to be feeding. Some anglers look for the deepest slough they can find, and then fish smack in the middle of it. That's not a good idea. Drum tend to feed where water is entering or leaving a slough, or along its banks, but seldom in the quiet water in the middle. Look for fast-moving water where baitfish are having trouble getting through. It is here that big drum meander up to struggling finger mullet and other bait and gulp them down without the effort of a chase.

Smaller red drum will occur in the same places, but usually at different times. They also occur along jetties and groins and in the channels near bridge stanchions.

Red drum under twenty-five pounds are regarded as edible, while the little ones in the two-to five-pound class are considered delicacies. The giants are generally released, although coastal Carolina natives do use them in fish cakes and stews. Small ones have white, chunky meat that is easy to get at, while big ones are rather coarse and protected by huge, platelike scales that are difficult to get through. Most anglers release large red drum.

In both Carolinas, the minimum keeper size is fourteen inches. The possession limit for red drum thirty-two inches and up is two fish in North Carolina and one fish in South Carolina.

CHOPPER BLUEFISH

Big bluefish are the most important game fish of the Atlantic coast. More anglers fish for and catch them, over more coastline, over a wider range of inshore to offshore waters, and over a longer season, than any other sport fish. If you have ever been one of those anglers, you know why.

Blues are voracious. They will hit anything that moves and most things that won't, will chop schools of baitfish to pieces leaving gore and flesh in the water, stuff themselves like angler fish with elastic bellies, chase food up onto the beach and even strand themselves in the process, and engage in feeding frenzies like packs of sharks.

Looking like scaly jacks, bluefish are in their own fish family (Pomatomidae), unrelated to anything else. Their razor-sharp teeth can cut through all but the heaviest monofilament, and given enough time they can probably part that too. They can severely lacerate, even maim, your fingers or hands, as many fishermen have learned the hard

41

way. A blue drives its jaws toward each other until the teeth meet, and won't let go until it has completed its bite.

Most anglers fish with wire leaders and avoid shiny hardware. Blues are attracted to metallic glare and to the color red, and that leads us to the best methods for catching them from the surf.

When blues are not seen, anglers put cut bait on a single-hook bottom rig. The standard rig is tied with a three-ring swivel, one ring leading from the shock leader, another to the sinker. The third ring is tied to a six- to twelve-inch segment of 40- to 60-pound wire. Coated, black, braided wire is popular and resistant to kinks. Uncoated, brown, single-strand wire is easily twisted during a fight and then becomes useless. Heavy duty (80- to 100-pound-test) silver-colored, single-strand wire is used by some anglers, but the glare causes numerous false strikes on the wire instead of the hook. A size 8/0 to 9/0 long shank hook is crimped to the wire, and its shaft buried in a large, red or yellow (red is more effective) foam float. This is called a Fireball Rig on the Carolina coast, and it catches a lot of big blues. The colored float serves as an attractor of bluefish, while simultaneously keeping the bait off the bottom, out of reach of crabs and olive snails. Olives will drag bait under the sand for feeding, which is another reason for frequently checking your hook. Any kind of bottom rig will catch bluefish, but seldom as well as the Fireball Rig.

The best baits for Fireball Rigs are large chunks of cut fish. Many guides like a one- by two-inch chunk of whole mullet or menhaden. You can also use a whole finger mullet or anything else available. Big blues are not fussy. It is important to check your bait often, for a juicy, fresh bait will put out its own odor, and blues can smell a bait a long way off.

Blues in the surf are often marked by wheeling, diving birds. The type of bird may indicate the kind of fish. For example, small groups of terns suggest little tunny (false albacore) feeding on anchovies or silversides. Diving pelicans suggest mullet, and that could mean big blues. When you see huge flocks of diving gulls well off the beach, that almost always means big blues feeding on mullet or menhaden. At such times, anglers stand around anxiously watching the progession of the birds, hoping that the school of blues will move into casting range. The wise angler pays attention to any concentration of gulls, feeding or not.

When gulls group up and hover quietly over a defined area, there are probably non-feeding blues below. If they are close, cast a lure into that quiet water below them. A wounded, fleeing baitfish is the trigger that starts the pandemonium. Once a feeding blitz begins, any large, silvery, heavy casting lure will work. The best lure on the Carolina coast is a big Hopkins spoon with a single hook, with or without a bucktail. If you love the crash of a surface hit, try a popping plug, especially after dark. Too light and bulky to cast very far, poppers work effectively only when the fish are close in. During a blitz, some lures will inevitably be lost as hooked fish attract others that bite rigging up past the protective wire.

There are several ways to land a big bluefish in the surf. You can use the waves to wash them up on the beach, or you can gaff them. If you want to release your blue, it can be safely and easily lifted by grabbing the tail stem. Under no circumstances should you put your hand in the mouth of a live bluefish.

Bluefish occur in many parts of the world. There are blues off northern and southern South America, off North Africa and in the Mediterranean, off southern Africa and Madagascar, and off Australia. These are all separate stocks.

Our Atlantic and Gulf coast fish consist of two or three separate populations. One group spawns in the spring off South Carolina and Georgia at the edge of the Gulf Stream. Another stock breeds during the summer off the Carolinas and Virginia. A smaller third group breeds in the fall south of Cape Hatteras. The larvae from these spawns spend different amounts of time at sea before heading inshore.

Young fish have preferences and tolerances unlike those of the adults. They enter low-salinity estuaries and even travel up into virtual fresh water. They tolerate colder temperatures than adult fish and range farther northward.

During most of the season, from early spring through the summer and into the fall, small bluefish are abundant all along the Carolina coast. Giant chopper blues appear on the North Carolina coast in April from their wintering grounds offshore from the capes. After they arrive, they spread out, some moving southward but the bulk of them migrating northward, mostly well off the beaches, leaving the coastal waters to their smaller siblings. The northern migrants will return in November and December, once more congregating at the capes. Sometime in early or mid-December, they will move offshore once again to overwinter near the edge of the continental shelf.

In warm winters, groups of these fish will make the short run back to the Carolina beaches in pursuit of baitfish, but their presence inshore is hit-or-miss.

The abundance of coastal big fish varies from year to year, giving rise to reports of cyclic appearances and disappearances. In going over data, testimony, and hearsay published in Bigelow and Schroeder's *Fishes of Chesapeake Bay* (1928), Smith's *Fishes of North Carolina* (1907), Jordan and Evermann's *Fishes of North and Middle America* (1896), and Goode's *American Fishes* (1888), plus a few other works, the following picture emerges of the "cyclic" bluefish.

Bluefish are almost always around. No author reports that they are absent at the time of writing, only that local fishermen have said that bluefish were more abundant in the past. Several old works state that the fish never ranged into the Bay of Fundy or eastward to Bermuda. Yet Beebe and Tee-Van, in their *Field Book of the Shore Fishes of Bermuda* (1933), state that blues are there, but uncommon. And Liem and Scott, in *Fishes of the Atlantic Coast of Canada* (1966), explain that young bluefish are quite common in northern climes, but associated with years of warm temperatures and the co-occurrence of large schools of menhaden. Mr. R. Edward Earll, as reported in Goode's *Natural History of Useful Aquatic Animals* (1884), made some important remarks about visits to the North Carolina coast from 1877 to 1880. According to

Earll, "It seemed that there is no reason to believe that the fish have permanently left the coast, or that they are even so scarce as is at present claimed, for the men have fished with little regularity, and have gone a short distance from the shore, while the bulk of the blue-fish may have been farther out."

And according to Liem and Scott (1966), "During the summer they remain in waters where the temperature is 58° F or higher. The immature sizes sometimes swim close to shore and these appear to be the only ones that stray far north."

Finally, Bigelow and Schroeder (1928) gave reports by fishermen complaining that bluefish were very rare in the late 1920s, with very few caught. Yet, these authors provide landing data for Chesapeake Bay showing that blues were the seventeenth most abundant fish landed during this same period.

In every case, it appears that fishermen or their children or grandchildren report that blues are currently not as abundant as they used to be, but the landing data do not bear out these claims. Limitations on how often and where fishermen fish seem to provide the only factual basis for the fancy.

What does appear cyclic is the occurrence of big, chopper blues close in along our coastline. There are two possible explana-

44

tions. First, big bluefish may be offshore during years when they are not found on the coasts. It is true that in years past we had almost no high seas fishing effort and virtually no reporting system. This possibility can be investigated if the big blues once more disappear from our shores and modern offshore vessels manage to locate them. Second, it is possible that big chopper blues periodically die off because of some natural catastrophe. That catastrophe would have to be something that affected only the large fish, for we have already seen that small blues are always around.

A principle of epidemiology is that infections spread best when the population becomes very crowded. But that principle does not provide a satisfactory explanation, since blues of some size are almost always abundant somewhere. If they are scarce above Cape Cod, that's likely due to a cold season or lack of forage fish. In any case, bluefish are probably never scarce off the Carolinas. What we need as an explanation is an infectious disease that affects fish when they get old, rather than when they are crowded.

Such a disease has recently been discovered. Myers, Sawyer, and MacLean, writing in the *Journal of Parasitology* (1977), described their studies of a rather obscure, parasitic proto-zoan called *Henneguya*, which lives in the heart of bluefish. Rare in young blues, it becomes increasingly common in larger bluefish. In very heavy infections, heart muscle destruction becomes obvious to the unaided eye. The authors remarked that heavily infected fish fought as hard on hook and line as uninfected fish, and they didn't know if the parasite seriously debilitated big blues. That may have been the wrong question, or the right question in the wrong context.

In our discussion of flounder, we saw that infections of young fish during a vulnerable time in their lives could take a devastating toll. That was because very young fish cannot initiate an immune response. In the case of bluefish, we should take note of the fact that in the very old, the immune response begins to deteriorate. We might speculate that, in a population of heavily infected, very old bluefish, a year of extremely cold offshore temperatures might have a similarly devastating effect on giant blues.

This is speculation. We don't know whether *Henneguya* is a parasite that should cause concern. However, its incidence in bluefish should be continually monitored so that we will have a biological parameter to consider if the fish suddenly decline. And if they should suddenly "disappear," we must be ready to search for remnants and conduct intensive water quality and biological studies to find a correlation.

The size of bluefish has been a matter of speculation. Liem and Scott report that blues can get up to 50 pounds, but provide no evidence. We have no hard data on fish in this size range. For many years, the all-tackle IGFA record was 27 pounds. In 1979, a 29-pound fish was caught, close to the current all-tackle IGFA record of 30 pounds. Fish over 20 pounds are commonplace, and several close to 25 pounds were taken in the fall of 1984. Many of these "giants" were normal-length fish that had stuffed themselves with spotted sea trout and mullet until they were as round as bloated puffers. It seems clear, however, that we don't know how big bluefish can get, for the current population consists of the largest adults in memory, and we don't have good records for the distant past, when other giants were said to have been around.

Let's hope that we don't have to enjoy them only in our memories. In response to recent foreign interest in exploiting our bluefish stocks, the South Atlantic and Mid-Atlantic Fishery Management Councils have produced a fishery management plan (FMP) for bluefish to control harvests and assure that commercial fishermen and sportsmen alike continue to have access to a fair share of a protected stock. That's good management and portends good fishing for years to come.

16 lb. 9 oz. and 19 lb. 7 oz. Bluefish
Caught by Garry Oliver at Oregon Inlet, North Carolina (Photo by Margie Rogerson, Dare County Tourist Bureau)

STRIPED BASS

Critics never fail to roar that the striped bass is the most thoroughly researched and least understood of all game fish, usually in an effort to curtail further expenditures on a fish that seems to eat up tax money as fast as it can be allocated. Well, the critics are wrong. Striped bass (*Morone saxatilis*) are very well understood indeed, and we are making progress in managing a species once beyond any hope of saving.

Sportsmen in North and South Carolina can take stripers or "rockfish" in several coastal rivers during the spring spawning runs, but most anglers head for the major lakes during the remainder of the year. Kerr Lake on the North Carolina–Virginia border and the Santee-Cooper Lakes in South Carolina are the principal reservoirs holding natural spawning populations. Other lakes in the two states are stocked by state agencies and also offer fine striper fishing year round. The methods and places for catching inland stripers and their management regimes are totally different from the problems and solutions related to coastal striped bass. This book is solely concerned with our Atlantic coast stocks.

We don't have very many stripers along Carolina beaches these days, and despite the hazy recollections of equally hazy experts, it's not at all certain that we ever did. Famed sports angler S. Kip Farrington, Jr., in his 1949 classic, *Fishing the Atlantic*, detailed striped bass fishing techniques in northern states, but when it came to the Carolina coast, he restricted his surf fishing report to the pursuit of red drum. Surely, had stripers been important game fish here in those days, he would have described local techniques, if only for comparison with the methods used elsewhere.

In fact, we do have striped bass along our beaches and near the points of the capes in early spring and midwinter, but these fish are not all the same stock and do not often come close enough to shore for sportsmen to enjoy.

Striped bass exist as several independent stocks along the Atlantic and Gulf coasts. From north to south, separate groups of fish spawn in different major estuarine rivers and migrate along the coastline for varying distances from their home rivers each year, depending on water temperatures and the availability of food. In the far northern reaches of the Atlantic Coast, the principal stock appears to be the Hudson River fish, a major population that has been maintaining itself very steadily for the last decade and shows no indication of declining. Those fish are loaded with Hudson River pesticide residues, resulting in restrictions on their capture and sale for consumption. This situation has affected relations between sport and commercial interests, with the New York Department of Environmental Conservation in the middle. NYDEC is attempting to make the best use of considerable data, and it is constantly expanding the data base upon which it makes its decisions. For example, it reached a thirteen-million-dollar settlement with a group of five New York State electric utility companies that requires the industry to set up and maintain a hatchery for striped bass; to monitor populations of breeding stock, eggs, and larvae in the Hudson; to schedule shut-down maintenance operations for periods coincident with spawning runs; to leave research goals and expenditures in the hands of an independent commission of scientists; and to continue studies of the effects of heated effluents from the power plants on early life stages. The settlement also requires the utilities to make sophisticated engineering alterations on their river water intake structures to minimize damage to stripers and other fish and calls for constant monitoring of their effectiveness and of other environmental parameters that might influence striped bass success in the Hudson.

To the south, the next important population is native to the Chesapeake Bay. That the bay itself is dying from pollution is widely known, and efforts to clean up the bottom and to limit further degradation from chemicals, siltation, and stagnation has not produced any increases in striped bass so far. Bringing back large numbers of striped bass requires: (a) a major spawning; (b) survival of the eggs and larvae during their early periods; (c) protection of the growing fish during the next few years so that they are killed neither by pollutants nor by fishermen; and (d) protection of the potential breeding stock those new fish represent. Despite federal funding for an interstate management plan for striped bass, the individual states are as variable as fishermen in their responses to the plan and in their efforts to clean up polluted coastal waters.

A good spawning year depends partly on the weather. Major spawnings often follow upon severe winters combined with very wet and protracted springs. That combination produces a long spawning season, and it is now known that baby fish produced late in the breeding season will make up the bulk of the year class. If that is interesting, it's also valuable information for management. It means that we must have a large number of breeding fish so that spawning can be extended. One fish producing half a million eggs is not as good as five fish producing one hundred thousand eggs each over time. It means we need a 24-inch minimum size for striped bass along

60 lb. Striped Bass
North Carolina State Record – Caught by Catherine Willis at Cape Point
(Photo by Ray Couch, Dare County Tourist Bureau)

the entire East Coast in order to assure that all fish get a chance to spawn at least once before they are available for harvest by either sport or commercial fishermen. It means that striped bass should be protected from harvest during their spawning runs and on their spawning beds. It means that commercial and sport interests should be spending more time learning about the biology of striped bass and less time fighting over their shares. It may mean a total ban on the sale of striped bass, a creel limit on top of the size limit, a closed season, closed waters, and perhaps, a closed year.

It is the Chesapeake Bay fish that are important to North Carolina coastal fishermen, for it is these fish that migrate south in the winter to bed down in the waters off Cape Hatteras. Here, commercial fishermen seek calm days in midwinter and venture out to the deep waters south of the cape, setting drop nets (sunken gill nets) on the bottom in hopes of finding the overwintering fish. Sometimes those fish come in close to the beaches, and haul-seiners operating from a small boat and a pickup truck fill boxes and barrels with thirty-pounders, to the dismay of recreational fishermen. As often happens with sea trout, the stripers on the beach are taken in numbers by netters while completely ignoring baits tossed by anglers.

There is a little-known population of striped bass in the Albemarle-Pamlico Sound area of North Carolina. Taken during much of the year by commercial and local recreational fishermen from small boats, these fish appear to spawn in the Roanoke and other nearby rivers of the Tar Heel State. The state of North Carolina has been expanding a stocking program to place fingerling hatchery fish in the headwaters of many of these rivers in hopes of bringing back strong natural populations. Unfortunately, commercial interests have been netting these fish almost as fast as they grow, and such interests have considerable clout with state politicians. Some commercial dealers were recently embarrassed when a 1985 "sting" operation resulted in the arrest of a number of them for knowingly purchasing striped bass that were illegally netted from inland lakes for resale as "legal" coastal fish.

The native Albemarle-Pamlico stripers occasionally work their way to Oregon and Hatteras inlets in North Carolina, but their wanderings generally go unnoticed. The inlets are virtually unfishable from boats during the violent winters, and few anglers brave the beaches during such cold weather. Should Oregon Inlet be stabilized by capped jetties, that will change. Fishermen will continue to fish the inlet into the winter, and the jetties will almost certainly attract both the Albemarle-Pamlico fish and the Chesapeake Bay fish.

Striped bass also spawn in coastal rivers of South Carolina, and when the Santee-Cooper system was dammed some years ago, the fish trapped in the upper river maintained themselves as a breeding population by continuing to spawn above the newly formed lake. This was the first indication we had that striped bass could survive and complete the entire life cycle in fresh water. The phenomenon repeated itself in the upper reaches of the Roanoke River (Dan River) with the construction of Kerr Lake.

Shore fishing for striped bass is a cold business. The best time to go is December, but a warm period in January might also bring the fish close to the beaches. Look for the fish at the capes and inlets in midwinter.

Inlet fishing is best from a bridge or jetty, if available, on a strong, outgoing tide. Cape fishing might be good on any tide. The best times are often sundown or at night. The water should have a chop but be clear and clean, rather than murky, and should be loaded with baitfish.

Casters in the Carolinas prefer big Hopkins spoons or very large popping (blunt-headed) plugs fitted with a treble hook and white bucktail. Plugs might be blue and white or white with a red head. Other lures should have both the weight for casting and a bit of red somewhere. An eighteen-inch length of heavy, forty- to sixty-pound-test monofilament suffices as a leader unless big bluefish are in the vicinity, and then sixty-pound-test wire is preferred. Snaps and swivels are always kept to a minimum and painted black.

Lures are worked right behind and then through the largest waves or the roughest surf on a beach, or parallel (as much as possible) to structures.

Meat baits can also be used for striped bass, or they can be used to sweeten an artificial lure. Popular meat baits are a whole crab, whole bloodworm, or live eel on a bottom rig. Dead eels can be rigged for casting, with one hook through the nose and out the gullet and a second hook midway back and out the belly. Rigged eels are especially effective from jetties.

More information on current striped bass research is available from your state marine fisheries people and your congressmen. Ask for the free current annual report of the *Emergency Striped Bass Research Study*, published jointly by NOAA-NMFS and the U.S. Fish and Wildlife Service. A major document summarizing knowledge of striped bass resulted from the Fifth Annual Marine Recreational Fisheries Symposium held in Boston, Massachusetts, and is available from the International Game Fish Association (IGFA) as MRF-5. For additional information on this and other sportfishing legislation and research, write the National Coalition for Marine Conservation and the Sport Fishing Institute. For addresses, see the Appendix.

PART II: FISHING FROM STRUCTURES

Groins and jetties are great concentrations of boulders differing in size, use, and location.

Groins are intended to stabilize eroding beaches and are placed in a series. Sand tends to accumulate on the upstream side of a groin and disappear on the downstream side, resulting in a scalloping of the beachfront. If located precisely, a groin can protect a particular, small segment of beach property, but invariably at the expense of adjacent land. Thus, a groin placed immediately downcurrent of a beach house will cause a buildup of beach in front of the house but rapid erosion of the beach in front of a neighbor's house just downstream of the groin. In the absence of coastal management, the entire beach suffers. That is what happened to the coast of New Jersey, where today myriad groins extend practically into the coastal towns, and the beach has virtually been eliminated as a place for surf fishing. Instead, fishermen fish off groins, which they call (incorrectly) "jetties." A more serious consequence of building groins is the destruction of beach-stabilizing sand dunes, which are rapidly eaten away by the locally concentrated erosion. The result is the exposure of the entire barrier island to overwash and the risk of new inlets being incised.

Jetties are intended to stabilize inlets that are migrating or shoaling, and they must be constructed in pairs. Jetties must deal with three problems: the bypass of sand along the beachfront, the alteration of the sandbar at the head of the inlet, and the inlet channel itself. Because jetties, even more than groins, significantly alter beaches, some system must be incorporated to displace sand to a downstream location. This might be the use of a bypass slurry pipe (still experimental) or simple hopper dredging from one side to the other. During the early years following jetty emplacement, the natural sandbar that occurs off the mouth of the inlet will dissipate, altering natural transport of sand along the coast. The channel itself will probably require maintenance dredging.

Jetties and groins are artificial rocky shores. They enhance the abundance and variety of fishes by providing attachment sites and hiding places for many kinds of marine life. Other creatures in turn then live upon their bodies as epiphytes (plants) or epizoans (animals). You've seen those squiggly white lines on oyster shells; they are the tubes of epizoan worms (*Sabella*) that can live only on something hard. The spaces between the rocks fill with silt, dead vegetation, or other materials, and burrowing worms and other creatures take up residence in the nooks and crannies.

While enhancing feeding opportunities for sandy shore fishes like red drum and flounder, groins and jetties also provide habitat for rocky shore fishes that might not have occurred here otherwise, such as black sea bass, black drum, Atlantic spadefish, sheepshead, tautog, and gag grouper. Open water (pelagic) game fish such as striped bass, bluefish, king mackerel, and amberjack regularly patrol jetties and groins for the abundant baitfish concentrations they attract in their lees.

Perhaps jetties and groins do the most good when they are destroyed, in which case they continue to function as artificial reefs but are no longer capable of enhancing erosion.

As northern fishermen have long known, groins and jetties are wonderful places to fish but can be dangerous. The so-called "jetty jockies" of the northeastern states have developed skills for clambering out on rock piles and dealing with the dangers of slipping on seaweed or being cut off by a rising tide. "Creepers," such as Walt's Walkers, are widely used rubber overshoes with sharp cleats that cut through the seaweed and grab the granite boulders. Creepers won't provide a safe grip if the seaweed is in several layers, and in any case they are an aid, not a solution, to groin walking. Long-handled gaffs are essential for groin fishing, doing double duty as walking sticks and props for the unsteady angler.

There is no substitute for common sense. Thus, jetty and groin fishermen know the times and heights of the tides like their own birthdays, and they won't get caught on the high far end of a jetty when the lower middle becomes submerged on a rising tide. They usually don't fish alone on an unfamiliar rock pile, for a slip can result in broken bones or being caught in a crevice. When you read about a lone angler taking a monstrous striped bass from a groin at night, you can be sure that he has fished there for years and knows every hole, every unstable rock, and every algae-covered slippery surface.

In response to recreational angler concerns, the Army Corps of Engineers has been constructing modern jetties with flat, asphalted walkways. These "capped" jetties are often equipped with guard rails and offer fishermen access to deep channel water, strong currents, and fishes very different and often larger than those normally available from a sandy beach. The south jetty at Murrells Inlet was capped in 1980, and both of the jetties proposed for Oregon Inlet will be capped.

Bridges have always been favorite fishing locations, but not enough of them provide fishing space to the public. Fishing from bridges is generally illegal in the Carolinas where the roadway is not separated by a railed walkway. In years past, local municipalities funded pedestrian walkways, but planning for recreational fishing catwalks was considered wasteful. That's not as true today as in the past, but it is still a problem.

Bridges offer some of the same advantages as jetties in the abundance and diversity of rocky shore fishes, the occurrence of strong currents and deep water, and the attraction of big predators. They are better than jetties for safety and in being positioned directly over a channel. The disadvantages of bridges are their extreme distance from the water (except in causeways), which precludes the use of hand gaffs; the tendency of the channels to become

highways for tackle-fouling refuse; and the inadequacy or absence of catwalks.

Some of our coastal bridges are heavily fished and well known for excellent catches. The Herbert C. Bonner Bridge over Oregon Inlet is famous for big gray sea trout and large sheepshead. Today, the catwalk over the north end of the bridge looks down on marshland, the result of shoaling and sedimentation around the stanchions. At the south end, the catwalk is narrow, but adequate for pulling a small wagon, and heavily fished. As the inlet continues to migrate southward, the deep channel will move closer to the catwalk. Along the south shoreline, the beach is now strongly riprapped to retard further erosion around the already weakened stanchions, enhancing the fishing even more.

The SR 406 Bridge over Fripp Inlet is heavily fished for sharks and big drum. It has no catwalk, and passing traffic makes this location less than perfectly safe.

The many low causeway bridges over the sounds of the Carolinas are usually overlooked by all but local fishermen, as tourists bypass them in their singleminded migration to the ocean beaches. Yet, the bridges over our low-salinity sounds provide outstanding fishing for big flounder and abundant sheepshead, with occasional tautog and black sea bass congregating around the virtually unfished stanchions. Many scuba divers have commented on the abundant sheepshead and striped bass around the causeways over Pamlico Sound, while on an average day there might not be more than one small boat per mile of bridge. Unfortunately, few of the causeways provide catwalks for fishing anywhere along their lengths.

The small highway and railroad bridges that crisscross our major ports are rich in small game such as pigfish, pinfish, and spot, but in the spring they become outstanding locales for big cobia, especially along the stanchions abutting the swiftest channels. The Beaufort-Morehead City railroad bridge is one of the hottest cobia locales in North Carolina, but only people in boats can take advantage of that fact. Fishermen are usually excluded from small bridges when they're operational and carrying traffic. Then, when the bridges become old and useless, they are condemned and fishermen are still excluded! That's changing. Today, many municipalities are maintaining old bridges as fishing piers, rather than removing them for scrap. The principal draw here is the abundant small game. The angler who wants big fish can usually find them too. It is simply a matter of working the

deepest and swiftest waters with big baits tied onto strong tackle. To catch big fish, you have to fish specifically for them and then be prepared to handle them when they hit. Bridges offer many opportunities for just such action.

The coastal plain of North and South Carolina provides ideal beach structure for the insertion of fishing piers. Vast, shallow, sandy shores slope into deeper water. Scattered patches of grasses, mussel-encrusted rocky outcrops, and overgrown wrecks litter the shoreline just behind the waves.

Of a total of 137 piers on the Atlantic and Gulf coasts, one-third are located in the Carolinas, from Kitty Hawk to Hunting Island. There are 35 piers in North Carolina and 9 in South Carolina. For the rest of the seaboard, there are just 3 in Maine, 1 in New Hampshire, 10 (mostly wharves) in Massachusetts, none in Rhode Island, 2 in Connecticut, 3 in New York, 9 (now mostly amusement parks) in New Jersey, 3 in Delaware, 1 in Maryland, 9 in Virginia, 3 in Georgia, 34 in Florida, 5 in Alabama, 2 in Mississippi, none in Louisiana, and 8 in Texas.

Piers are typically 400 to 1,000 feet in length. There are only a few state park piers in our area. Most piers are privately owned, charging a three- or four-dollar admission fee. They are open sixteen to twenty-four hours a day from April through November and are equipped with a bait and tackle shop, rest rooms, a grill, snack bar, or restaurant, one or two fish-cleaning sinks, benches, lights for night fishing, and official weighing scales. They provide equipment rentals and tackle repairs, and some of them provide motel or camping accommodations.

They all have rules, and some have special fees. Only a few allow shark fishing, and then only at night, while most piers never permit it. Most allow king mackerel fishing (sometimes at a premium fee) at any time in reserved areas, while others allow it only on weekdays, and some don't permit it at all. Determine the rules in advance, for it is very easy to find a pier somewhere that will accommodate your interests.

The forty-four ocean fishing piers of the Carolinas are well equipped for every kind of shore and nearshore fishing. While flounder fishermen flip strip baits or live killies along pilings near shore, other anglers bait up with bloodworms for spot or sand fleas for pompano. Further out, anglers with casting gear throw jigs at small bluefish or Spanish mackerel or sink shrimp for croaker. At the end of the pier, flinty-eyed regulars keep watch over two-rod rigs for the strike of a cobia, king mackerel, tarpon, or amberjack. At night, sharkers with basketball-sized reels keep silent vigil for a lumbering sand tiger or cruising lemon.

A list of all the piers in our area appears in the accompanying table.

TABLE 1. FISHING PIERS OF THE CAROLINAS

Kitty Hawk Pier, Kitty Hawk, N.C.
Avalon Pier, Kill Devil Hills, N.C.
Nags Head Pier, Nags Head, N.C.
Jennette's Ocean Pier, Whalebone Junction, Nags Head, N.C.
Outer Banks Pier, South Nags Head, N.C.
Hatteras Island Pier, Rodanthe, N.C.
Avon Pier, Avon, N.C.
Cape Hatteras Pier, Frisco, N.C.
Triple S Pier, Atlantic Beach, N.C.
Oceanana Pier, Atlantic Beach, N.C.
Sportsman's Pier, Atlantic Beach, N.C.
Morehead Ocean Pier, Atlantic Beach, N.C.
Iron Steamer Resort, Atlantic Beach, N.C.
Indian Beach Pier, Emerald Isle, N.C.
Emerald Isle Pier, Emerald Isle, N.C.

TABLE 1. FISHING PIERS OF THE CAROLINAS—continued

Bogue Inlet Pier, Emerald Isle, N.C.
New River Inlet Pier, Surf City, N.C.
Paradise Pier, Surf City, N.C.
Ocean City Pier, Surf City, N.C.
Scotch Bonnet Pier, Surf City, N.C.
Barnacle Bill's Pier, Surf City, N.C.
Surf City Pier, Surf City, N.C.
Dolphin Pier, Topsail Beach, N.C.
Jolly Roger Pier, Topsail Beach, N.C.
Johnny Mercer's Pier, Wrightsville Beach, N.C.
Crystal Pier, Wrightsville Beach, N.C.
Carolina Beach Pier, Carolina Beach, N.C.
Center Fishing Pier, Carolina Beach, N.C.
Kure Beach Pier, Kure Beach, N.C.
Yaupon Pier, Yaupon Beach, N.C.
Ocean Crest Pier, Long Beach, N.C.
Long Beach Pier, Long Beach, N.C.
Holden Beach Pier, Holden Beach, N.C.
Ocean Isle Pier, Ocean Isle, N.C.
Sunset Beach Pier, Sunset Beach, N.C.
Cherry Grove Pier, 34th Avenue North, East Cherry Grove Beach, S.C.
Holiday Inn Pier, 27th Avenue South, North Myrtle Beach, S.C.
Second Avenue Pier, 210 North Ocean Boulevard, Myrtle Beach, S.C.
Springmaid Pier, Myrtle Beach, S.C.
Myrtle Beach State Park Pier, Myrtle Beach State Park, S.C.
Surfside Beach Pier, 11 South Ocean Boulevard, Myrtle Beach, S.C.
Kingfisher Pier, Ocean Boulevard, Garden City Beach, S.C.
Crosby's Fishing Pier, James Island, S.C.
Hunting Island Pier, Hunting Island, S.C.

EQUIPMENT FOR FISHING FROM STRUCTURES

The equipment for pier fishing is different from that for sand beaches, rock jetties, or narrow bridge catwalks. Piers offer room for major equipment and transportation and the opportunity for innovative techniques.·

PIER CART

A wagon or cart marks the full-time pier angler, the specialist who needs lots of equipment to do his best. The cart allows him to travel the thousand feet between his car and the end of the pier in one trip without wearing out.

Building A Pier Cart

Beginning pier anglers use a toy wagon or a surplus supermarket shopping cart. These can be built upon to create wonderfully complex trailer rigs. PVC tubes can provide rod holders. The dimensions of the wagon or cart determine the size of cooler and tackle box and the limits of carrying capacity.

Advanced pier anglers construct portable wooden sheds, beginning with a dolly and

Pier Cart

working up around it with framing and plywood. Wheels are oversized, and there may be drawers for tackle instead of space for a tackle box. PVC rod holders are bolted to the outside, and there may be hooks for carrying buckets, gaff, net, or other large gear. There are no rules for how to build a pier wagon, and your enthusiasm is the only limitation.

GAFF

A pier gaff is simply a weighted gang hook used to lift big fish from the sea. Coastal tackle shops sell them, but you can make one in a home workshop.

Building A Pier Gaff

The key to a good pier gaff is at least four prongs (since the wind will spin it around) and a lot of weight to keep it straight down. Add a one- to two-inch tube filled with lead to the shaft of the gaff, and keep the prongs well out and curved broadly upward.

A chain on your pier gaff will protect the rope from shark bites and provide snagging holes if the gaff is dropped or pulled away. The rope should be strong and of a very wide diameter so that it is easily held and hauled. If the diameter is too narrow for easy hauling, add knots every few feet to provide grips. A gaff is necessary for sharks, cobia, tarpon, king mackerel, amberjack, and big bluefish. It can be a big help when your rod goes overboard!

LANDING NET

Pier nets are sold at coastal tackle shops for about $10. Made of a four-foot-diameter metal hoop and two-inch-mesh string, the net should be fitted with a heavy hauling rope, of the type used for a gaff. Nets are used largely for big flounder, red drum for live release, sea trout (weakfish), and any other fish that looks as if it might drop off or pull free.

COOLER

A cooler should not be made of light, cheap plastic foam, which will break under a heavy load or blow away in the wind. A heavy, solid plastic or metal-frame cooler with a drain plug will last for years and is a good investment. Coolers should be equipped with plenty of plastic bags for storing bait and fish apart from the ice and food, and one or two decapitated plastic milk jugs for fillets, baited rigs, and a host of other uses. You should also include a wooden cutting board small enough to carry inside the cooler.

PLASTIC PAIL

Some anglers forego a cooler and put all their tackle and bait, and the fish they catch, into a five-gallon plastic bucket. Available from fast food restaurants and some tackle shops, those pails have a lot of uses, but insulating fish from heat isn't one of them. They are useful as tackle boxes for a single activity, such as float fishing for king mackerel, or bottom fishing for sharks. Cut a hole in the lid and run 60- to 150-pound-test monofilament line between the lid and the handle to keep your top from blowing away.

CAST NETS

Nylon monofilament cast nets in different mesh sizes will reward the persistent fisherman with valuable live bait. When used from a pier, the net should be attached to an excess of heavy nylon line and constantly checked for frays. The pier end should be looped around the wrist before throwing. Quarter-inch-mesh nets will catch silversides, anchovies, finger mullet, baby bluefish, and little herring close to the beach. One-inch-mesh nets are good for big mullet and menhaden near the end of the pier. Net diameter is important, with bigger nets more likely to encircle a lot of fish than small ones. Skill is more important, however, so don't buy a net bigger than you can throw. You can always trade up as you develop skills. Look for nets with strong construction, and avoid imports. Betts makes a nice series of nets at reasonable prices.

BAIT BASKETS

Two kinds of live-bait containers are used on piers and bridges. For small baitfish, Woodstream makes floating minnow buckets constructed of molded plastic or galvanized tin, standard equipment with small-boat bass and flounder fishermen. They are also useful for holding killies, finger mullet, and silversides when suspended into the water below on a heavy, nylon line. Metal containers are more sturdy than plastic, able to withstand beating against the stanchions or pilings.

A different kind of container is required for holding live menhaden, adult mullet, or ten-inch bluefish for king mackerel baits. You can purchase a collapsible wire basket with spring-loaded upper and lower lids for about $5. Some anglers construct big menhaden buckets from five-gallon plastic pails, milk cases, or other materials.

PIER, BRIDGE, AND JETTY TACKLE

FISHING RODS

You'll need a variety of rod and reel combinations for structure fishing. Note that many privately-owned piers allow each angler two rods, while some piers charge you a ticket per rod.

Big conventional surf sticks are used by red drum fishermen to heave heavy sinkers and big baits great distances. Pendulum casting is standard on Carolina fishing piers, requiring very stiff rods to throw one-pound payloads.

If you're a sharker, you'll want a fifty- to eighty-pound-class conventional boat rod with butt gimbal and a roller tip-top guide, but this rod won't be used for anything else.

For king mackerel fishing from ocean piers, big surf spinning rods are most often used to lay out the anchor line. The fighting rod is often a short, fast-taper, conventional live bait rod or boat rod. Daiwa and Eagle Claw make several models, but prices vary greatly, and many anglers construct their own from components.

Long, fast-taper, medium-weight surf spinning rods are good all-around rods, capable of handling small to large game in experienced hands. Short, one-handed spinning rods are used to catch small game such as pompano, spot, small bluefish, Spanish mackerel, flounder, croaker, and other fishes for consumption or for king mackerel bait. Graphite rods are getting cheaper and are popular with sheepshead and flounder fishermen. Among the more attractive new graphite models are the Berkley LR-30 Lighting Rod and Shimano QGC-2652 Quickfire.

REELS

Conventional antibacklash casting reels such as the Garcia Ambassadeur 10,000 CA or the Penn Magforce 970 are used by red drum fishermen. Less expensive and still popular is the Penn Squidder. King mackerel fishermen often use conventional reels on short, fast-taper, live bait boat rods, as their smooth drags are very responsive.

Sharkers prefer 9/0 to 12/0 Penn Senators, although less expensive 6/0 Senators are used by some sharkers and king mackerel fishermen. On several occasions, big tarpon or amberjack have all but stripped 6/0 reels.

Small conventional baitcasting reels are generally not used on ocean fishing piers because less expensive spinning reels will do the job and are easier to clean and service.

Large-capacity spinning reels are used both for king mackerel anchor line rods and for direct fishing. Very popular are the Penn 850-SS, Daiwa BG-90, and Shakespeare 2200-080.

The variety of small spinning reels suitable for one-handed rods or medium weight surf spinning sticks is enormous, and they are all good if kept well greased (do not use light machine oils) and washed free of salt and grit. Silicon lubricants can damage and lock up hard nylon gears in some of these reels, so stick with organic lubricants. Some anglers mix a small amount of STP oil additive with automobile grease, but petroleum jelly will work very well.

LINES

Sharkers prefer 80- to 130-pound-test dacron line because of its resistance to stretch and aging. Most other anglers use high-quality monofilament lines from 8- to 30-pound-test, with 17-pound-test line the most popular. The wise angler changes monofilament line completely on every reel once a season, while king mackerel fishermen may change lines two or three times in the course of a summer. Although the outer line shows the most obvious signs of wear and aging, the inner line also takes a beating and should be discarded when servicing a reel.

ANCHORS

The anchor sinker is a four- to eight-ounce lead weight with a brass ring for casting and a group of long, flexible wires molded into the sides that provide extraordinary purchase in soft sand. It is a British innovation. King mackerel fishermen used to construct them, but these sinkers are now commer-

Anchor Sinker

cially available on the Carolina coast and are well worth the extra cost.

OTHER TERMINAL TACKLE

The remaining terminal tackle used by pier, bridge, and jetty fishermen is the same as that used by surf anglers.

CASTING FROM STRUCTURES

The type of casting you do from a pier, bridge, or jetty depends on where you want to place your bait and the kind of tackle you are using. Red drum fishermen at the seaward end of a pier or jetty use long-distance casting to throw heavy payloads of bait and lead weight, while king mackerel fishermen on ocean piers need to cast their anchoring weights as far as possible. Both use the pendulum swing. This sidearm casting method takes a lot of room and the cooperation of everyone around. Watch for tourists before proceeding, and always warn your companions when setting up the cast. "Watch out" or "Low bridge" are not nearly as effective as "I've never done this before."

The fact that a pier is a platform in space offers some casting advantages. For casting long distances with a two-handed surf stick, use an overhand cast when the area is clear of pedestrians. For casting a one-handed rod, an underhand flick will often do the job. Do not cast heavy weights on big rods underhanded. Should the reel lock, that terminal tackle may fly back onto the pier deck and hit someone. If your reel should lock on an overhand cast, the terminal gear will break off harmlessly and fly away or swing under the pier.

BAITS FOR FISHING FROM STRUCTURES

ARTIFICIAL BAITS

The most widely used artificial baits on Carolina fishing piers, bridges, and jetties are very different from those used by boaters or inland fishermen, or even those used by structure fishermen in other states. Although they will be discussed under the specific fish headings, a few types are standards and should be mentioned here. These are the sinking plug-jig hybrids (e.g., the Hildebrandt Jerk Jigger and the Gotcha) and the metal squidding spoons (e.g., the Hopkins No=EQL or 7S, and the Conner Z1H). Lightweight spoons, small bucktail jigs, and plugs are not used on fishing piers, as they either cannot be effectively cast into the wind or don't sink quickly.

NATURAL BAITS

Many natural baits are used by Carolina anglers, while other baits standard to the north or south are not seen here. Baits conspicuous by their absence are cut crab (used on northern jetties for tautog), clam (used in Virginia for black drum and further north for other kinds of fish), and live eels (used in New England for striped bass and on the Gulf Coast for cobia).

Mullet

Most every size of mullet, from three-inch finger mullet to foot-long adults, is available at all tackle shops, freshly iced or frozen. Frozen mullet are useless. Fresh mullet can be used as entire heads or scaled fillets for red drum, cut into small chunks for croaker, or even cut into meaty cubes or strips for flounder. Finger mullet are used whole for flounder and red drum. Because mullet become soft in a matter of hours even when iced, freshness is essential. Live finger mullet castnetted from a pier, or whole adult mullet snagged with a Hopkins lure out of a school, are among the best baits you can get.

Small Bluefish

Not sold in tackle shops, small blues can be caught on Jerk Jiggers and Gotcha lures from structures and used as live baits for king mackerel or cut bait for bottom fish.

Menhaden

Three species, Atlantic menhaden, yellowfin menhaden, and Atlantic thread herring ("grass shad"), can all be cast-netted or snagged with treble hooks from structures and used as live king mackerel baits or cut up for bottom fishing.

Other Fish

Just about any fish you catch can be cut up and used as a fresh bait. Flounder belly is said by many to be the premier bait for flounder. Shark or ray skin strips are also excellent flounder and gray trout baits and will catch bluefish. Any fish you don't intend to eat or cut up for bait should be released, but don't eliminate any fish as potential bait just because you haven't seen it used that way before.

Squid

Frozen squid are sold in all bait shops, but fresh squid, available from some seafood markets, are superior. Three-inch by quarter-inch strips of cleaned squid mantle (covering the eye and tentacle section) are standard flounder bait but will also catch gray sea trout (weakfish), black sea bass on hard bottoms, and croaker. The squid's tentacle section should not be discarded, as it makes a great bait for large, doormat-sized flounder.

Worms

Live bloodworms are expensive at twenty-five to forty cents each, but half-inch pieces are the best of all baits for spot. These worms have nasty pincers, so cut off the head. Earthworms can also be used for spot, and are cheaper. Black lugworms and other new baits are being offered in some areas in an effort to develop a market, but their effectiveness is not yet clear.

Shrimp

Frozen shrimp are standard baits and will take almost all bottom fish if moist and fresh. Old freezer-burned shrimp or those that have been allowed to warm and spoil are useless. Some of the southern tackle shops sell live shrimp, outstanding bait for speckled trout, gray sea trout, and flounder. They are often not nearly as expensive as worms, but don't use them if small bluefish are around.

FISH CAUGHT FROM STRUCTURES

SPOT

People come to our piers and bridges to catch spot more than any other fish, and for good reason. Ranging from Massachusetts to Mexico, spot are especially abundant in the Carolinas and Virginia. According to the National Marine Fisheries Service (NMFS), the commercial catch is about 10 million pounds a year, and the U.S. recreational catch is 2.1 million pounds a year.

The recreational estimate is probably too low. For example, if we estimate for the Carolinas alone an average catch of 25 spot per day at ¼ pound per fish times 200 people per ocean pier times 44 piers times 3 days a week times 8 good weeks, we get an annual catch of 1.32 million pounds, which is within three quarters of a million pounds of the NMFS estimate and doesn't even include Virginia, Georgia, Florida, or the Gulf Coast, or the Carolina sound piers, beaches, and bridges, or the fish taken by boat anglers.

According to NMFS, spot don't do well in markets compared with other fish because of their fishy flavor (compared with northern species such as porgies and cod), poor freezing qualities (because of the strip of brown meat along the lateral line), and small size. In fact, local Carolinians think that they freeze just fine and that the meat is delicious. But how can you take gourmet advice from people who freeze ungutted fish in paper milk cartons?

Spot feed all season inside the sounds and along the ocean beaches. In September and October, the fish in the sounds join those on the beaches. The one- and two-year-old adults fatten up and prepare for their winter spawning migration, many of them sporting bright yellow bellies as their hormones begin to run.

The fall spot run is protracted, with new fish appearing and others moving offshore for breeding, so that the size of fish being caught changes from day to day. Meanwhile, the breeders offshore are having a great time making little spots. The eggs hatch at sea, and the baby fish, barely a thirteenth of an inch long, slowly wash back toward shore to enter the estuaries in January, February, and March. They have a rough year in store for them.

The baby fish migrate up to the head of the estuaries, where the water is least salty. As they grow at their winter rate of perhaps a millimeter a week, they move down into the more saline and deeper estuarine waters. During this time, many are eaten, starve, or die of other causes. If there is too much freshwater runoff that year, many more will die. The survivors grow faster when spring arrives. If the summer is hot, growth will be slowed while natural mortality continues, and the average size may decrease. The few survivors that mature represent only a tiny fraction of the original number of larvae that entered the estuary the year before. At a year old, the survivors are ready to join the ocean spawning population.

The average keeper spot (there is no minimum size, but most anglers throw back fish too small to clean) is two years old, nine inches long, and a quarter- to a half-pound in weight. A foot-long spot would weigh over a pound and be a rare three- to four-year-old.

Spot are invertebrate-eaters, which accounts for their sweet taste. They feed mostly on tiny marine crustaceans (isopods, amphipods, ostracods, shrimp, crab), mollusks (small clams and snails), and worms. They pick food off the bottom and from the water close to the bottom.

Fishing for spot means picking the right location (the "right spot") and giving them a bait they just cannot live without. Spot find a half-inch segment of bloodworm irresistible. Some fishermen use red wiggler earthworms, which are cheaper. Spot are seldom in the shadow of a pier or bridge, but may be next to it. Usually they are just a short cast away. Use a two-hook bottom rig with small (number 4 to number 1) hooks, a light rod, light line, and a light sinker. The rod should not be hauled back to sink the hook but lifted just enough to put solid tension on the line. The fish will hook itself.

Some old-timers freeze whole spots in milk cartons filled with water, and only clean them after thawing. Never accept dinner invitations from these people! Most anglers cut fresh fillets from spots, while others simply slice one slab off each side and call it a fillet. The strips of meat should be iced quickly and frozen with water in plastic bags, one meal to a bag. Despite the views of NMFS, I've never heard of anyone throwing out spot because they had picked up a bad taste in the freezer. Spot are usually served as breaded, pan-fried fillets with a squirt of lemon juice.

CROAKER

The Atlantic croaker is one of the most abundant shore fish in the Carolinas. Many are caught in the surf, but more are caught from bridges and piers. Commercial fishermen prefer them to spot because of their larger size, but croaker are not as tasty, and that's probably due to the fish in their diet.

From Massachusetts to Mexico, croaker have been reported to eat just about everything. The Gulf Coast Research Laboratory in Mississippi identified eighty-three different food items in their stomachs. In North Carolina, for example, croaker ate skinny, shrimplike crustaceans even when meaty commercial shrimp were around. Inside estuaries they gorged on commercial and non-commercial shrimp, crabs, worms, clams, and small fish. Outside in the ocean, they ate more clams and fewer worms, which probably indicated what was there rather than what they preferred. They tend to eat more fish in the fall when most of us catch them, and that's probably why they taste fishier than spot, which aren't fish-eaters.

Croaker grow slowly, maturing at age three or four when about nine inches long. A foot-long fish weighs just over a half-pound, and a twenty-inch fish weighs about two pounds. They get up to about four pounds, but that would be an old fish.

They breed offshore in the winter like spot, and the larvae swim and drift to the estuaries for early growth. Croaker sometimes mix with spot, but usually the schools remain separate. The young fish have slightly different salinity preferences.

Croaker are cyclical, and their numbers are currently a little below average. Older fish dominate the ocean recreational catch, while the commercial pound net fishery of the sounds continues to take younger fish.

Croaker often feed in deeper water while spot tend to occur close to the surf line. And while both fish can be caught at night, croaker seem to be more active night feeders around ocean fishing piers.

The croaker feeds by forming its jaws into a tubelike apparatus and then extending that tube down onto the bottom like a siphon. In an aquarium, it looks like it is pushing a vacuum cleaner.

Croaker are usually caught on two-hook bottom rigs baited with shrimp, squid, or cut mullet. They love bloodworms, but that expensive bait is unnecessary. Like spot, they are usually a short cast away rather than straight down or underneath the structure. Hook size should be number 4 to number 1, but a hungry croaker will accommodate larger sizes. Because they form narrow feeding tubes much smaller than their mouths are capable of opening, the pieces of bait many people use are much too large. Given a large bait, a croaker will pick it up on the end of the tube and run, and it will be virtually impossible to hook. Give it small bits of bait that can be sucked inside, and you'll hook all you want. As with spot, hook them by just lifting the rod to tighten the line. That mouth tube is very flimsy, and hooks will tear free readily.

Croaker have sharply spined gill covers that can abrade your hand unless you wear a glove while dressing them. They are usually filleted like spot. Because of their larger size they can also be dressed as butterfly fillets or simply scaled, gutted, and beheaded for broiling, poaching, or steaming. They are very nice pan-fried with butter, parsley, and lots of almond slivers.

Large croaker can be poached in a steaming vegetable broth. The broth is made with one onion, one stalk of celery, one carrot, salt and pepper, a bay leaf, half a teaspoon of any dried herb (but especially fennel), two tablespoons of vinegar, all in two quarts of water. Cook the vegetables gently until they are slightly soft and lose their bright color. Place the entire dressed fish in this simmering court bouillon for ten minutes per inch of thickness. When done, remove the fish and strain the broth, discarding the vegetables. Melt some butter in a small pot and, when it bubbles, add a heaping tablespoon of flour. Mix well to create a paste, and then add some of the strained broth, continuing to mix vigorously. That will give you an exquisite sauce with almost no trouble and no fancy ingredients.

WHITING

Three species of whiting (sea mullet in North Carolina) are caught from our ocean piers and bigger bridges. Popular surf fish up north, where they're called king whiting or kingfish, whiting can be caught at any depth, with the largest fish usually hooked in deeper water at the far end of the pier or mid-channel below a bridge. Big whiting are hard-fighting fish and often need to be netted up to the deck. Whiting are discussed in more detail in the section on surf fishing.

SNAPPER BLUEFISH

Small bluefish are popular with small game fishermen who like to eat them, and king mackerel pier fishermen who want them as live baits for their float rigs. Little snapper blues are usually caught on Hildebrandt Jerk Jiggers, Gotcha plugs, small Hopkins metal squids, or other heavy lures that cast far and sink fast. The usual procedure is to find gulls diving on a feeding school and then to throw right into the baitfish at the surface. Even when there are no diving birds, some anglers will catch snappers on artificials. Throw to the same place and you will, too. Little blues also take cut bait on the bottom and during the retrieve. They are attracted by any kind of movement and the color red.

Small blues are abundant during the summer. Unlike their gray-meated, fishy-tasting big brothers, little snappers have delicious white meat with just a hint of oil. Snappers are usually gutted and pan-fried whole. They are also excellent when smoked, having just enough oil to pick up the smoky flavor of burning hardwood.

GRAY SEA TROUT

Gray trout (*Cynoscion regalis*) are the most common of four kinds of "sea trout" in the Carolinas. There are two major breeding populations of gray trout on the Atlantic coast. The northern population, known as weakfish or squeteague, is centered off New York. The southern population, known as gray trout or summer trout, extends from New Jersey to South Carolina.

Gray trout occur in Carolina waters almost year-round. They are caught from late spring to early fall in holes located within inlets and channels. In early winter they begin cruising the outer sloughs off ocean beaches, where commercial trawlers, but not surf casters, can reach them. At this time, roving hordes of chopper bluefish may drive them onto the beaches. As the water gets colder, they move offshore.

Gray trout breed inside the sounds and bays from May through July. The eggs hatch in two or three days, and the larvae grow rapidly, leaving the estuaries in the fall for offshore wintering grounds. They return in the spring and spread out along the coast, the older and larger fish traveling farther northward and southward. They live three to five years, but seven-year-old and older fish have been found. The average Carolina fish is fifteen inches long and a pound and a half in weight, which is about a fifth the size of the average Chesapeake

Bay fish. We also have schools of six-pounders, but they are less common. The largest gray trout from our area are the South Carolina state record 11-13, the North Carolina state record 14-14, and the world record 19-0 from Virginia. All the big fish are females.

Gray trout feed on fish, shrimp, crabs, squid, and anything else that comes their way. Their front canine teeth are excellent weapons for gripping or slicing baitfish. They are often caught on squid strips or live killies by people flounder-fishing in channels or from bridges. They will hit cut mullet still-fished on the bottom; Hopkins, Sting Silvers, or Bagley's Salty Dawg (all metal jigs); or Gotchas and Jerk Jiggers (both sinking metal plugs) cast out and slowly retrieved. If bluefish are around, and you want only trout, use a plug with a blue head and white body, tie a wet fly about a foot back on a dropper, and work the combination lure slowly in arcs over the bottom. Because their jaw tissues are flimsy, big trout should be netted up to the deck. Anyone who has ever tried lifting a big trout by the fishing line has gotten an instant explanation of the name "weakfish."

Nobody ever catches too many trout, and none of them are wasted. Gray trout are excellent eating and fat enough to broil or smoke. Their bones are few and soft, so there is no point in filleting them.

SPOTTED SEA TROUT

The spotted sea trout, speckled trout, speck, or winter trout (*Cynoscion nebulosus*) ranges from New York to Texas and is most common in the southern part of our region. Unlike gray trout, specks do not move offshore. They travel about inside sounds and bays, usually occurring in grass beds and inshore channels.

Our Carolina specks are different from Florida specks, and it appears that the Atlantic coast has numerous, independent, and quite different populations that behave almost like different species. Our northern fish, for example, spawn in the cool spring, while Gulf of Mexico fish spawn in the heat of summer.

Spawning takes place in deep parts of bays. The bigger the female, the more eggs produced. A 15-inch fish will produce about 15,000 eggs, while a 20-inch fish will produce ten times that number. A really big fish, about two feet long, will produce between half a million and a million eggs. Females get larger than males, grow faster, and live longer.

After spawning, the eggs sink toward the bottom and hatch about forty hours later. The larvae move into the shallows, where they feed on plankton in the thin film of water over the silt. Growth is rapid. The fish attain six inches the first year and are a foot long by the third year. Afterward, they add about two to three inches a year. Males live about six years and females eight, but ten-year-old fish have been found. Old females leave the schools to become solitary fish. Specks average two to four pounds, and the maximum size is believed to be around seventeen pounds. The large fish are all females.

Food consists of anything they can catch, but they have a strong preference for live shrimp and big fish. Small specks can be taken at night on a live minnow or shrimp fished under a float, while the big ones often hit a live pinfish, spot, or bluefish. The best daytime lure for specks is a MiroLure fished in clear water, but at times they will also hit Hopkins, Conners, Sting Silvers, Salty Dawgs, lead-headed bucktail jigs, and even spoons.

Always use a pier net on big specks, for their mouths tear easily, and their flesh is readily torn by a gaff.

Small and medium-sized spotted sea trout are highly regarded food fish. Delicious fried, broiled, baked, or poached, the sweet white meat is superior to that of gray trout. Large individuals may have in their meat flat, nervelike white bands that end in a little ball. These are the lar-

vae of *Poecilancistrium robustum*, pretty little tapeworms that grow up and take on adult form only when the speck is eaten by a carcharhinid shark. They are perfectly harmless to people and probably very nutritious, but the unsightliness of these "spaghetti worms" has depressed the commercial market in big southern specks.

SHEEPSHEAD

Some fish come and go without rhyme or reason. Fishermen attribute the ups and downs in fish populations to natural cycles or environmental stresses, but nobody really knows the reasons for the changes.

Fluctuations in bluefish, striped bass, and Boston mackerel populations have occurred in our lifetimes. Are some cycles so long as to be unrecognizable? Perhaps the sheepshead can shed some light on these questions.

The sheepshead, *Archosargus probatocephalus*, was first brought to the attention of scientists in 1792 when the ichthyologist Walbaum described it from specimens collected in New York. That was not unusual, as there were not many scientists working much to the south in those days.

The fish was recognized even then as a member of the porgy family (Sparidae), while the porgy we know today from the northeastern states was, at the time, a relatively little-known fish. The question is: was the fish common in New York in 1792, or did Walbaum perhaps find it in the famous Fulton Fish Market? Perhaps the existence of Sheepshead Bay, to the east of Coney Island in Brooklyn, might shed some light on the question of sheepshead distribution. It's possible that the sheepshead was so common at the end of the 1700s that a New York bay was named for it.

Sheepshead
Caught by Henry Coble at Bogue Pier

G. Brown Goode, writing in *American Fishes* (1888), reported:

This fish has never been known to pass to the north of the sandy arm of Cape Cod, and its northern range is at present somewhat more limited than it was eighty years ago. In the records of Wareham, Massachusetts, they are mentioned as having been somewhat abundant in 1803, and in Narragansett Bay there is a tradition that they began to disappear in 1793, when the Scuppaug commenced an increase in abundance. In 1871, E. E. Taylor, of Newport, testified before the U.S. Commissioner of Fisheries, that his father caught sheepshead in abundance forty-five or fifty years previous. In 1870 and 1871 the species was coming into notice in this region, though neither at that time nor since has it become common. On the south shore of Long Island it is quite abundant, and in New York harbor and its various approaches, at times, may be taken in considerable numbers.

Goode went on to describe the general range of the sheepshead and its importance to fishing from Montauk Point at the east end of New York to the coast of New Jersey and south into Chesapeake Bay. He noted that it was reported as common in the Carolinas and abundant from southern Florida to Mexico.

Today, the sheepshead is regarded as a southern fish, difficult to entice onto a hook, and associated with hard bottom structure from the Carolinas to the Gulf of Mexico. A lot of this is not exactly true.

Sheepshead occasionally occur on hard structure in Virginia waters and are not rare in Chesapeake Bay. Their range extends from Massachusetts to Yucatan, with a subspecies (*Archosargus probatocephalus aries*) extending in brackish waters south to Brazil.

Breeding occurs in the spring in sandy areas, and the eggs drift away to hatch in about two days. The growth rate is unknown, but the fish get up to two feet long. IGFA doesn't include the sheepshead among its listing of game fishes for record status, so no official world's record exists. Scientists have estimated the maximum size at perhaps 20 pounds. A 7- or 8-pound fish is a big sheepshead in our area. The largest North Carolina fish is the state record 18-7 monster caught thirty miles off Carolina Beach on a rocky reef in a hundred feet of water. The largest South Carolina fish was 15-4, taken from a jetty in Charleston.

Sheepshead occur wherever they can use their incisorlike buck teeth to pick shellfish off hard structures. Delighting in barnacles, mussels, and slow-moving crabs, the sheepshead is a grazer upon attached animals and totally oblivious to fish as food.

The best places to find barnacles, mussels, and similar foods are off the bottom and in strong currents. Here, siltation is not a problem and filter-feeding shellfish thrive. That is why sheepshead can be found along pier pilings, bridge abutments, stanchions, rocky outcrops, jetties, and other places of strong current. Sheepshead also occur where other fishes cannot find food, such as within the hotwater discharge canals of power plants, where they graze on the barnacles that grow attached to submerged concrete pipes and walls and sunken tree roots.

If the range of sheepshead has radically altered in the past couple of hundred years, as suggested by Goode, to what may it be attributed? A few ideas come to mind.

Goode referred to sheepshead declining at about the same time as the increase in scuppaug (an old name for our common northern porgy or scup). A member of the same family, the porgy also has a predilection for shellfish, but it is far less selective. Rather than living in association with a structure, porgies travel widely in vast schools and, like locusts, a passing horde can easily wipe out the local food supply.

The sheepshead is not a migratory fish. Its only movements are inshore and offshore for

73

spawning or to escape low winter water temperatures. It is not a rover. It occupies a home territory where it finds the food it needs. Any sheepshead fisherman can tell you that sheepshead are not all in one place. You have to find one here, catch it, and move on to the next likely structure. There may be one big sheepshead associated with two pier pilings in one location, and the next sheepshead will be found some hundred feet further on, associated with another group of pilings. On jetties, several small sheepshead may be in one localized area, but never a large number. Instead, they spread out to share the attached animal life covering the jetty, reef, or other structure. And here they stay. If their food supply is eliminated, they will starve.

Did the porgies starve out the sheepshead? Will the porgies ever decline, and will the sheepshead ever spread northward again?

We could speculate what might happen if porgies were overfished, or if the New York and Mid-Atlantic bights were cleaned up of pollutants. I remember one year long ago when spot came into Sheepshead Bay in great abundance and were virtually a new fish to everyone who caught them. It happened only that one time. Water temperature? A big mid-Atlantic population spreading out to the north? Nobody knew. Perhaps it could happen again, with sheepshead.

Fishing for sheepshead is an art. If you cannot see them, then you have to pick out where they are likely to be. That means finding a hard structure, well off the bottom, in an area of constant (not intermittent) strong current. Often overlooked are the areas of current inside the sounds, where the water appears calm and uninteresting. Nonetheless, a lot of Carolina sheepshead are taken in inside waters. The sides of a jetty are good, the end even better, and the top best of all. For bridges, mid-channel is best, alongside a concrete post or wall. Pier pilings are good, especially out over deeper water.

The standard rig consists of heavy leader material connected to a minimal-size sinker that you can control in the current, and a short, heavy monofilament or light wire leader running from the sinker to a thick, short-shank 1/0 to 4/0 hook. Some anglers use graphite baitcasting outfits for sheepshead because of the extreme sensitivity of this tackle.

Bait must be shellfish. Peeler (soft shell) blue and whole fiddler crabs are good, as are fresh barnacles scraped from nearby structures and smashed open with a hammer. The best all-around bait by tradition is the pregnant sand flea, identified by

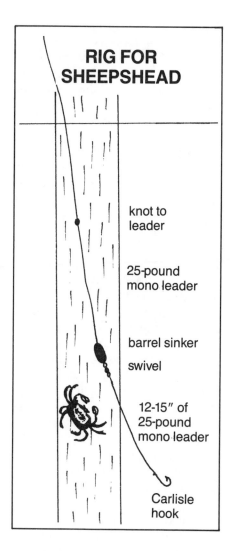

RIG FOR SHEEPSHEAD

knot to leader

25-pound mono leader

barrel sinker

swivel

12-15" of 25-pound mono leader

Carlisle hook

BLACK SEA BASS

The black bass (a local Carolina name) or black sea bass (*Centropristis striata*) is an inshore, rocky-bottom fish caught around bridges, jetties, and those piers adjacent to rocky bottoms. A member of the sea bass and grouper family (Serranidae), its only inshore relative is the gag grouper.

Black sea bass range from Cape Cod to Florida, but their center of abundance is New York to South Carolina. They are protogynous hermaphrodites, maturing when four years old as females and later changing into males. Not all individuals change sex, but the odds are that fish longer than one foot are six-year-old males. Older males develop iridescent blue humped backs.

Above Cape Hatteras, black sea bass inhabit water fifteen to twenty (up to a hundred) feet deep during the summer. When winter comes, they aggregate offshore at 200- to 500-foot depths, where commercial fishermen exploit them. South of Cape Hatteras, we have a different and quite extraordinary phenomenon. As temperatures drop, all the black sea bass and subtropical triggerfish, snappers, and southern porgies inhabiting these shallow, rocky reefs leave the inshore waters to overwinter close to the Gulf Stream some thirty to sixty miles offshore.

the spongy orange roe on its underside. Fished against structure, the fisherman must wait until he senses the gentle inquisitiveness of a sheepshead's probing lips. And just before he feels the fish, he sets the hook!

The inshore reefs are then invaded by temperate zone fish, such as tautog, coming down from the north.

In our area, black sea bass spawn far offshore during April and May. The eggs float at the surface, hatching about five days later. Until they are well developed, the tiny baby fish will remain at sea, growing and developing pigmentation. With increasing size, they move into shallow shore habitats for the summer but they will leave again in the fall. As the fish grow older, they spend each year farther from shore.

The best places to find sea bass on Carolina shores are jetties. Here, a bank sinker helps keep your standard two-hook bottom rig from getting caught in the rocks. The 3/0 hooks are baited with squid, clam, fish, or anything else both large and likely to remain on the hook. Sea bass have huge maws, and the smallest juvenile will engulf an enormous bait. If you want to keep your fish, remember that the minimum keeper size for black sea bass caught in South Carolina is eight inches.

The sea bass is among the first fish to spoil if not gutted promptly and packed in ice. Its liver leaks acrid bile fluid into the meat upon death, and no sea bass should be dressed "tomorrow," no matter how tired you are.

Properly cared for, the meat of a black sea bass is among the best the Carolinas have to offer. Especially suitable for steaming or poaching, it is an excellent choice for oriental dishes. Try this one, for example.

_____

You will need a soup bowl, a pot for steaming, a small frying pan, fresh garlic, ginger root, soy sauce, green onions, sugar, oil or chicken fat, and a can of chicken broth. Get a big soup bowl that will fit inside a large covered pot, put a half inch of water in the pot, put the bowl inside, and heat the water to a simmer. Mix two tablespoons of soy sauce, a half cup of chicken broth, and a teaspoon of sugar. Take a fresh sea bass with the head on (you can use a frozen one that has been allowed to thaw), and lay it inside the soup bowl. Pour the soy sauce mixture over the fish, and rub some inside the body cavity. Sprinkle finely cut-up green onions, including the ends, over the fish. Bring the water to a gentle boil, cover, and steam the fish for fifteen minutes per inch of thickness. Longer won't hurt, as sea bass meat doesn't overcook. Finely chop two cloves of garlic and a quarter-inch-thick slice of ginger root (don't use powdered ginger!), and brown them in a small frying pan on medium heat in three tablespoons of oil or chicken fat. Remove the sea bass to a serving platter. Pour the hot garlic-ginger oil over the fish (it will splatter!) and serve with plain boiled rice.

SPANISH MACKEREL

Heather Wadsworth had held the IGFA world record for Spanish mackerel since 1983, the year she brought a fish barely under 11 pounds to the wharf in Oak Bluffs, Massachusetts, which is far outside the normal range of the species. Because an old fishery report indicated that Spanish mackerel might attain a weight of 25 pounds, perhaps the people who identified the fish didn't worry very much about the similarity of Spanish mackerel to young king mackerel (which can have yellow spots when young) or cero mackerel (whose yellow marks are supposed to be more like dashes than spots). For that reason, the big Massachusetts fish, to me at least, had a cloud on its validity.

But that is the past, because the record has been smashed by a fish almost 20 percent larger from the waters of North Carolina, and its validity is undeniable.

Captain Woody Outlaw of Ocracoke was entertaining friends Bob and Lorraine Cranton from Avalon, California, on November 4, 1987, with a day of trolling on his charter boat, the *Sea Walker*. They were trolling with the usual gear for king mackerel, and within 40 minutes had put three fish in the box: two kings and an outsized Spanish that Bob had easily brought to the stern. Neither Captain Out-law nor mate Charlie Brown realized the fish might be a world record when Charlie handlined it into the ice box, and only later, back at O'Neal's Dockside Marina, did they realize what they had.

The big fish took a blue-and-white Sea Witch, sweetened with a strip of fatback menhaden on a 7/0 hook. The Shimano baitcasting reel, mounted on a Kuna rod, was loaded with a 30-pound-test Ande line.

Outlaw got pictures of the fish, which clearly exhibits the deep body and short, upturned-snout characteristic of Spanish mackerel. The big fish was 33 1/2 inches long and 16 1/2 inches in girth. Because Woody is a professional skipper who's caught cero mackerel before, he is well aware of the differences among all the closely related species.

The 13-pound-even fish is a new North Carolina state record, and the paperwork is being processed to get the fish certified as a new IGFA all-tackle world record.

There are several kinds of mackerel in the Atlantic, and the record seeker knows the differences among them. For example, frigate and bullet mackerels (*Auxis*) are merely bait-sized, never getting big enough to hit a rig. Boston and chub mackerels (*Scomber*) occur just north of our area, live only in cold water, and don't look anything like our traditional species. The mackerels in which we're interested are the king and Spanish (*Scomberomorus*). Kings (*S. cavalla*) have a lateral line that drops sharply to zigzag at about the middle of the body. Small ones have yellow spots on the side. Spanish mackerel (*S. maculatus*) at all sizes have brassy yellow spots on the side, an almost straight lateral line, and a black smudge on the front of the dorsal fin. The cero mackerel (*S. regalis*), which is so rare in our area that it is usually not even considered, resembles the Spanish but is larger and has one or two broken rows of bright yellow streaks (not spots) on its side.

There are two other species of *Scomberomorus* in the Atlantic. The Iberian mackerel (*S. tritor*) occurs in waters off Spain and Portugal, and the Brazilian mackerel (a Spanish look-alike) occurs in the South Atlantic.

Recent studies by the National Marine Fisheries Service Panama City Laboratory, the U.S. Fish and Wildlife Service Biological Services Program, and the University of the West Indies in Trinidad have given us a lot more information on Spanish mackerel.

Spanish mackerel migrate all along the East Coast from Maine to the Caribbean. They are replaced by the Brazilian mackerel to the south.

Spanish mackerel arrive off the Carolinas from April through June at the same time as small bluefish. Breeding in our waters takes place at the mouths of estuaries at night when the water warms to more than 72° F. The floating eggs hatch at night about twenty-four hours later, and the tiny larvae are only a tenth of an inch long. Even at this size, they have massive heads and sharp little teeth. They grow quickly, and by two months have attained an inch and three-quarters in length.

The fish remain close inshore all through their lives. At two or three years of age they are large enough to breed. Females grow faster and get bigger than males. The oldest ones examined were nine years old.

HOW TO KNOW THE SOUTHERN MACKERELS

King mackerel
Scomberomorus cavalla

Lacks black mark on dorsal fin; lateral line dips abruptly; no spots on flank of adult, but spots occur on flank of juvenile.

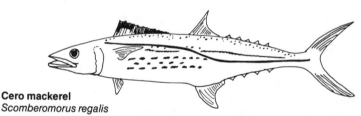

Cero mackerel
Scomberomorus regalis

Is rare; black mark on dorsal fin; lateral line dips gradually; about two broken yellow lines (may be elongated spots) on flank.

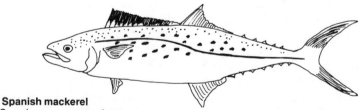

Spanish mackerel
Scomberomorus maculatus

Very common; black mark on dorsal fin; lateral line dips gradually; scattered, distinct round yellow spots on flank.

The commercial fishery for Spanish mackerel began sometime before 1850, and by 1880 some 86% of the U.S. catch was landed in Chesapeake Bay. That has now changed, and today Florida lands 92% of the total U.S. catch. The South Atlantic Fishery Management Council, in its Coastal Pelagics Fishery Management Plan, is attempting to distribute the sport and commercial catch more evenly along the entire coast and among all users. Gill net fishermen working open ocean waters just offshore in our area take about 87% of the commercial catch, but because their large-mesh nets select adult fish, there is little danger of overfishing the stock.

Sportsmen take Spanish mackerel inshore from boats, piers, jetties, and beaches at mid-depth or near the surface on rapidly retrieved small lures. Spanish mackerel are in our waters all summer long, but because they move about in schools, their occurrence at any one time and place is a matter of chance. Aware that Spanish feed principally upon anchovies, silversides, and small herrings, pier and surf fishermen use tiny white, gold, or silver lures tied directly to the monofilament line. Spanish are very hardware-shy, so don't use any snaps or swivels. Silver-finish Gotchas or Jerk Jiggers are effective, as are tiny Hopkins squids, 1½-ounce Sting Silvers, and Conner Z1H

lures. Large Spanish mackerel tend to be loners or occur in small groups, just like large kings. They will feed on larger baits, and many have been taken on float rigs. However, some small kings taken on these rigs have been confused with Spanish because of the yellow spots. In South Carolina, the minimum keeper size for Spanish mackerel has only recently been set at 12 inches fork length.

Spanish are superior to king mackerel as table fare, best served broiled with butter and slivers of almonds. They are excellent when smoked, having just the right skin, the right oil content, and the right thickness.

KING MACKEREL

I could see three of them cruising in a slow zigzag pattern just under the light chop. Several live bluefish baits began struggling fiercely against the hooks in their backs, trying to get away as the pack moved inexorably closer. The lead king mackerel headed straight for my live bluefish bait but passed beneath. Then the pack was gone. The blues settled down to their normal in-place swimming, but it took me quite a bit longer to unwind. I was pier fishing for king mackerel, and the excitement of seeing a pack of them among the baits is not for the faint of heart.

King Mackerel
Hatteras Island Pier, Rodanthe (Photo by Ray Couch, Dare County Tourist Bureau)

Most king mackerel taken from fishing piers are in the 15-pound class ("snakes"), but bigger ones are frequently hooked. The largest kings taken from our piers weighed 52-8 (Morehead Pier), 52-0 (Scotch Bonnet Pier), 50-0 (Barnacle Bill's Pier), and 49-0 (Springmaid Pier).

At most piers, the end section is reserved for serious king fishermen. Novices are helped if they use the right equipment and take advice from the old hands. People who insist on fishing with inappropriate gear are usually invited to leave. Hits are few and far between, and there is no room for anyone whose rigging might cause someone to lose a fish.

Kings prefer warm, clear water, and while southern piers more often have the best water, these conditions occur often enough at northern piers to make king mackerel fishing worthwhile anywhere in the Carolinas.

About fifteen years ago, the one-rod balloon method evolved on Carolina piers. Today, we have a better technique, known as the two-rod or trolley-line method.

The basic king mackerel fishing outfit consists of three fishing rods, terminal tackle for two of them, a lure for the third, connector rigs, and a live bait basket. One of the rods is used to cast a heavy sinker known as

81

the anchor, another is used to catch the live bait, and the third rod's function is to hook and fight king mackerel.

The anchor rod and fighting rod are rigged separately and very differently, but they must be mated at the pier with a connector. Let's describe the connector first.

A connector consists of a ten-inch segment of monofilament line weighted in the middle with a barrel sinker. The ends are tied to a shower curtain clip and a hole in the handle of a clothespin. We'll see later how this connector rig works.

The casting or anchor rod is a surf stick capable of throwing a big weight a long distance. The reel is loaded with light line for maximum casting distance. The terminal rig consists only of a shock leader tied to an anchor weight. The anchor is a four- to eight-ounce sinker with metal prongs imbedded in the lead. It gives terrific purchase in the sand. You can also tie a large trailing treble hook behind an ordinary surf sinker to produce the same effect.

A long cast is made, and the line retrieved until the bottom has been grabbed slowly and strongly. Then the line is tightened until the wind makes it sing and the rod has a strong bend. Maintaining the very taut line, the anchor rod is now either lashed to the railing or its

King Mackerel Rig

butt is inserted into a rod holder on the railing, provided by the pier management. There it will remain for the rest of the day.

The fighting outfit must have plenty of line capacity and backbone. Most king mackerel anglers use conventional tackle, from 4/0 to 6/0 boat outfits loaded with 30- to 50-pound-test line, down to the new light anti-backlash reels on live bait rods. Spinning gear is preferred by some anglers but may be too light for the occasional big smoker king.

82

TWO-ROD KING MACKEREL (TROLLEY LINE) RIG

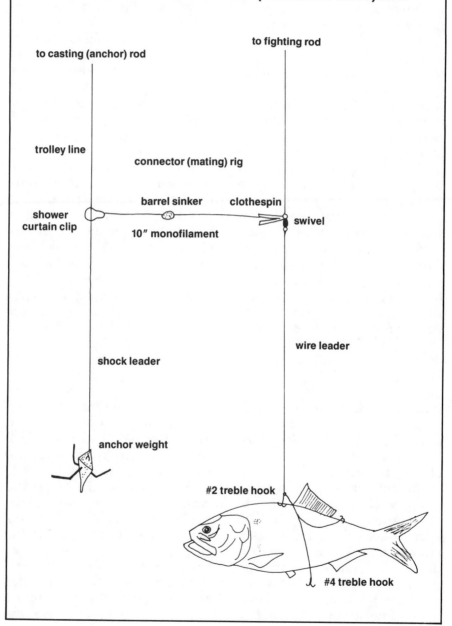

to casting (anchor) rod

to fighting rod

trolley line

connector (mating) rig

barrel sinker

clothespin

shower
curtain clip

10″ monofilament

swivel

wire leader

shock leader

anchor weight

#2 treble hook

#4 treble hook

No casting is done with the fighting rod, so no shock leader is needed. Instead, the line ends at a large snap swivel, to which the terminal rig will be tied.

Terminal rigs are made up in advance and stored coiled up in plastic sandwich bags. Uncoiling the rig, we see that it consists of three feet of twenty-five- to sixty-pound-test wire, with a swivel at one end and a cluster of treble hooks at the other. The hook arrangement varies from pier to pier and from year to year.

A common arrangement is a series of three small treble hooks, the first one wrapped directly to the wire leader, and the second and third hanging as two-inch and four-inch droppers either in series or in parallel. The shorter dropper will be inserted into the back of the baitfish, and the longer one either inserted into the underside of the rear of the fish or allowed to dangle freely in the water. All hook connections to the wire use large loops so that the hooks swing freely and cannot be wrenched off by a twisting fish.

The multiple small hooks will snag the king about its face or body as it whizzes by with half your baitfish. Snagging kings is more effective than trying to throat- or lip-stab them with a single hook. And while this terminal rig for kings is anathema to the International Game Fish Association, most Carolina anglers are more concerned with getting a fish than a record.

The best hooks and wire are bronze or black, for kings will avoid anything shiny. Berkley Tackle and Jeros Tackle make coated black wire leader materials. If all you have are nickle or steel components, the entire assembly should be sprayed with flat black paint.

Now it's time to get your bait. The most common bait is a ten-inch bluefish. A light, one-handed spinning rod is used to cast a small sinking lure such as a red-and-white Jerk Jigger or Gotcha, but you can also use bucktail jigs and small Hopkins squids. Small bluefish are almost always around piers in the warm months. If, for some reason, the small blues are hard to find, you can catch a small pinfish, grunt, or spot, any of which will do the job. Experienced pier fishermen use cast nets or snag rigs to capture menhaden, thread herring ("grass shad"), or mullet, which make the best live baits. Live baits are stored in a floating basket under the pier until needed.

Okay, we're all rigged up and have a live bait hooked to the trebles on the fighting outfit. It's time to slide it down along the anchor line, and now we see how the connector works. The clothespin jaws of the connector are used to grip firmly the upper ring of the swivel, where the fighting rod's line meets the terminal tackle. At the other end of the connector, the shower curtain clip is opened, passed around the line of the anchor rod, and closed again. At this point, the connector is gripping the fighting rod's terminal tackle and is loosely hanging from the anchor line. The fighting outfit's reel is either placed on free spool with the ratchet engaged, or (more often) maintained on a very light drag setting. The baited rig is allowed to slide slowly down the anchor line to the water, where the baitfish can start swimming again. In order to get the live bait as far as possible, you may want to vibrate the anchor line or lift the anchor rod and shake it vigorously. Everybody tries for maximum distance from the pier, since the outer rigs generally get hit first.

When a king crashes the bait, it usually hooks itself. Quicker than the eye can see, the forceful strike tears the swivel out of the jaws of the clothespin, and you are free to fight your game fish on a direct line, unencumbered by sinkers or floats.

Most regulars keep their reels on a very loose drag setting. The line being pulled through the water puts sufficient pressure on the fish (most of the time). Seldom will a king take more than two hundred yards, and the light drag prevents the king from wrenching free of the small treble hooks in its paper-thin skin.

Whether you get the fish or not, you will soon have to put another live bait out there, once again using a connector rig. When the fish struck, your connector broke away from the fighting rod and slid down the anchor line all the way to the bottom. It is not necessary to reel in the anchor. Simply pull another connector rig out of your gear bag and start over. At the end of the day, you can retrieve your anchor and all the connectors that you used.

If you have good tackle, and you want big fish at the right price, the piers of the Carolinas will give you a shot at a real thrill. Just be sure to seek the advice of experienced anglers, and take it. Then all you need to do is wait for a strike. You might get lucky.

King mackerel range from Massachusetts to Brazil and are abundant in the Carolinas, where they concentrate just offshore near Cape Fear and Cape Lookout but range out as far as the Gulf Stream for summer spawning.

The IGFA world record is a 90-pounder taken at Key West. The largest fish caught in our two states are the 79-pounder caught by Clifton Moss off North Carolina on November 11, 1985, and the 62-pound South Carolina state record, taken by J.

Brownlee off Charleston in 1976. A 62-pounder was taken off Southport, North Carolina in 1985. King mackerel may attain a weight of 150 pounds. Big ones are usually loners, often old female fish. They are caught more often around structures than in open water. Female king mackerel mature at three years of age and live to at least the age of eight. Although kings are the largest of the Atlantic species of *Scomberomorus*, there are Pacific species that get even larger.

Carolina king mackerel fishermen are very opinionated about the merits of various baits. We now have some evidence to settle the matter. A recent study of stomach contents of king mackerel caught in Onslow Bay, North Carolina, determined that their diet consisted 97.3% of fish. The fish distribution by species was 35% menhaden, 28% thread herring ("grass shad"), 14% spot, 8% pinfish, 5% bluefish, 5% mullet, and less than 5% all other fish combined. So the next time you're trying to determine which bait to use, remember that study.

The main populations overwinter off Key West, but there are always some kings in the Gulf Stream year round. After the charter boat season for billfish ends in late September, many skippers go out handlining kings commercially until the weather deteriorates.

The western Gulf of Mexico fish are a separate stock, so big

BRITISH ANCHOR, purchased in England

The U-shaped wires rotate and lock in place.

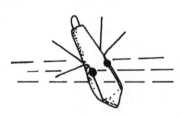

Left: Wires locked upward for purchase in sand.

Right: By giving a strong, steady pull, one can unlock the wires and cause them to fall backward, allowing retrieve of the anchor at day's end.

Florida landings don't necessarily portend a reduced catch as the Atlantic fish move northward in the spring. The South Atlantic Fishery Management Council sets annual catch quotas for commercial and recreational fishermen all along the coast in an effort to give everyone reasonably equal access. Should the council decide to close the federal zone to fishing, the state of South Carolina will support that decision by making it illegal to possess king and Spanish mackerel during any period when the federal zone is closed.

As the fish move into our waters in April and May, coastal towns from West Palm Beach to Morehead City begin promoting local king mackerel tournaments, two- or three-day affairs that draw fishermen from far and wide.

All summer long the fish will be within a few miles of shore, frequently heading inshore to the beaches for feeding around our piers. Some will even be caught in the surf. When fall puts a chill in the air and on the water, the fish move inshore after the schools of menhaden and mullet leaving the estuaries. They pile up in huge aggregations below the capes in preparation for the migration south. During September and October, pier catches will be excellent as long as the water remains clear.

The last tournament usually occurs in early October.

Kings may be steaked with a heavy butcher knife or cut into strip fillets. They are excellent smoked, barbecued, or grilled with lots of lemon and butter. A Mediterranean method is to wrap each steak or fillet in tinfoil with one slice of lemon; one bay leaf; a pinch of oregano; half of an onion; one tomato, chopped; one stalk celery, chopped; and one potato half or whole carrot. Preheat the oven to 450 degrees, and then bake for thirty minutes. The fish will steam inside the tinfoil without drying out and pick up all the flavors of the vegetables and herbs.

COBIA

When the calendar approaches Memorial Day, Carolina anglers from Currituck to Charleston and the mountains to the coast pack their bags, wipe their rods, oil their reels, and race to the piers and bridges for the annual arrival of the cobia (*Rachycentron canadum*). Vast schools will have been spotted offshore a month earlier, usually a one- or two-day phenomenon on the Atlantic coast. As the water warms into the low seventies, a few thirty- to fifty-pounders will be reported on the ocean piers. Memorial Day is usually when cobia fishing is at its peak. About a week later, the fish move offshore to the Gulf

Stream for spawning all through June, and then return to the beaches and inshore waters in July. In 1983 and 1984, the July period was the better one for catching cobia, and few fish were seen before then. On the Outer Banks, Jennette's Pier accounted for 59- and 75-pound fish, while to the north, the Kitty Hawk and Avalon piers reported 46 1/5-, 61-, and 73-pounders. The fish remain in our waters well into the early fall.

Breeding has been reported to occur from Chesapeake Bay to the Gulf Stream, but recent studies indicate that cobia eggs and larvae do not survive in low-salinity estuaries. In fact, the most important breeding ground seems to be the Gulf Stream. Dr. Hassler at North Carolina State University collected some two thousand eggs at the edge of the Stream during the month of June. Development of the large eggs and hatching occur rapidly, and the larvae immediately feed on plankton. By forty days of age, young cobia are large enough to eat guppies. Aging studies have shown that fish in the sixty- to seventy-pound range are seven to nine years old.

Related to sharksuckers (remoras) and nothing else, young cobia have patterns that are almost identical with those of their distant relatives. They also have the curious habit of following rays that are scouring the bottom, picking up what the rays have uncovered or missed. The similarity to remoras, which feed

49¹/₂ lb., 52³/₄-inch long Cobia
Caught by Glenn Groom at Nags Head Pier
(Photo by Margie Rogerson, Dare County Tourist Bureau)

on the parasites and leavings of sharks and big rays, is obvious.

Cobia occur in all the warm oceans of the world but are curiously absent from the Pacific coast of Central America. In the United States, they are common from Virginia to Texas and range northward to New Jersey. Because they travel extensively, each state has its peak period. In South Carolina it is usually mid-May, while in North Carolina it is two weeks later. Knowing where and when to go may seem pretty obvious, but some people catch cobia and others don't. Tackle is often the difference.

Cobia are big, strong fish and require heavy tackle. The North Carolina state record is 97 pounds, the South Carolina record is over 83 pounds, and an 87-pounder was taken from a North Carolina pier in 1982. A 94-pounder was the 1981 IGFA saltwater fishing contest top fish, and four cobia over a hundred pounds occupy the 20-, 30-, 50- and 80-pound-test IGFA line class records. The all-tackle champ is a 110-pounder from Kenya. An even larger cobia was taken in Florida in 1982 but disqualified from the record on a technicality.

Cobia usually run in mixed-size groups or harems of a large female and several smaller males. Most fish range from 10 to 60 pounds, with big females generally taking the first bait. Some big cobia taken from Carolina piers include five in the 70-pound class from the Oceanana, Avalon, Triple S, Surf City, and Jolly Roger piers, five in the 60-pound class from the Cape Hatteras, Sportsman, Paradise, Scotch Bonnet, Kingfisher, and Morehead Ocean piers, and plenty of fish in the 50-pound class. Few piers even bother to report those fish in the 30- to 40-pound range, and fish caught from bridges are seldom reported in the newspapers. South Carolina has recently set the minimum keeper size for cobia at 33 inches fork length.

Cobia hit any bait at all. Many a pier or bridge angler has been startled by the sudden appearance of a massive cobia head charging his little Jerk Jigger plug. Most of them are caught either on king mackerel rigs or by throwing a live bait to a fish spotted nearby. Cobia eat crabs, shrimp, squid, pipefish, dogfish, herring, eels, or anything else that tickles their fancy. Cut bait, live bait, and artificials are all successful. While live eels are generally regarded the finest of all cobia baits, they're hard to come by, and most of our pier and bridge fish are taken on live thread herring (grass shad), bluefish, pinfish, menhaden, croaker, or spot. While some baits do better than others, the bait makes not a bit of difference if the tackle is not strong enough to hold the fish once it is hooked.

The most common mistake is using tackle that is too light. Cobia are far more powerful than their weight alone would indicate. On even heavy tackle, the one word that best describes a cobia battle is *long*. They simply don't wear out, and fights of an hour or more aren't unusual.

Typical cobia tackle consists of a conventional saltwater reel loaded with twenty-five- to forty-pound-test monofilament line, a six-foot boat rod with plenty of backbone, and a pier gaff. Cobia are pier and bridge fish, seldom taken from the surf. The best reels are the large, anti-backlash ones. Favorites include the centrifugal Ambassadeur 7,000 and 10,000 CA and the Penn magnetic series, 970 and larger. You can also use non-casting reels with a 4/0 or greater line capacity. Spinning outfits are usually too light. The reel drags tend to slip while putting almost no pressure on the fish, and the rods are not stiff enough to budge or bother a cobia.

You can catch cobia with cut bait on the bottom but are more likely to pick up a shark, conger eel, or ray with that method. If you're rigged for king mackerel, you're ready for cobia. Most cobia are spotted at the heads of piers, where king fishermen are already rigged up and waiting.

But if a cobia is spotted where no rig is ready, the best bet is to throw a live bait at the fish.

A 5/0 to 9/0 short-shank hook is tied directly to ten feet of 60-pound-test monofilament leader, and the leader is tied directly to your line. Swivels and snaps interfere with casting through the guides. Your leader doubles as a shocker and must be very long because cobia will run along pilings and other structures and cut you off. If you've time to tie it, add a number 2 or larger dropper treble hook about six inches below the main hook. Both the main and dropper hooks should be inserted into the live baitfish.

Cast beyond and to the side of the fish and work the bait back slowly on the surface. If the fish refuses the bait, try placing it near that rascal on a float. A balloon is ideal in an offshore wind.

Above all, don't get nervous. If the cobia seems to be moving away, don't panic and recast trying to cut her off. Cobia near structures tend to remain there. The fish is more likely to be cruising around the structure than going away from it, so be patient and allow your bait to sit where it is.

It's a good idea to keep several live baits in the water at different depths and scattered around the pier or bridge. Cobia may not come up to the surface, feeding strictly on the bottom. Many cobia are caught by people with live bait rigs on the sides of the pier, having arrived too late to get a kingfishing spot at the end.

Unlike kings and other game fish, cobia seldom miss a bait. Even a small cobia has a maw eight to ten inches wide, and the bigger ones have almost a square foot of opening to throw around your live bait. If you fail to stick a cobia, it's because the hook was too small, the rod too light to sink it, or you hit the fish too soon. The mouth of a cobia is practically armor-plated with bone. It's best to let the fish run off with the bait some distance before striking hard. Go for a belly hookup.

The cobia might respond in any of several ways to the feel of the hook. Often it just sits there and then slowly moves off. Smaller ones are more likely to run. In any case, the fish will head for structure, and heavy and long leaders are about your only defense against a cutoff. Sometimes, particularly with light tackle, the fish will allow itself to be eased within gaffing distance. "Green" fish are never gaffed when you are fishing from a boat, as they have lots of fight left in them and can destroy everything in the cockpit. On a pier, it's a different matter. The fish might be pier gaffed, but it is a risky business. At the sight or touch of a gaff, the fish might panic and wrap around a piling or rush off faster than your drag can slip. It's good sportsmanship, and smart fishing practice, to induce the fish to move away for the fight. If you can wear it down in twenty to sixty minutes, that's the time to sink the gaff, and not before.

Cobia have excellent food qualities and should never be wasted. They are delicious prepared any way at all, but when smoked, they are comparable to sturgeon. Native Carolina anglers make a fish stew of the head, which is loaded with rich, yellow-white meat in glistening wet slabs. Prepare a simple vegetable broth, either fresh or from a can or package, and simmer the entire head for about an hour.

AMBERJACK

The jack family (Carangidae) is a worldwide group of two hundred species of oceanic and coastal fishes. Several jacks occur in our waters, including the delicious little pompano, its relative the permit, and the strange-looking rudderfish, lookdown, and bumper. Two of them, the amberjack and the crevalle jack, are large game fish likely to be caught from ocean piers on king mackerel rigs.

Amberjack (*Seriola dumerili*) range from New England southward and are our biggest jacks. Abundant offshore, the big jacks enter inshore waters

Large Amberjack

scales big enough) at 105 pounds. Then, in 1983, Jerry Hunt landed a 110-pound whopper on the Sunset Beach Pier, just above the North/South Carolina state line.

The IGFA world record is 155-10 for a Bermuda fish. The North Carolina state record is 125 pounds for a fish taken at sea off Cape Lookout by Paul Bailey. The largest South Carolina fish is a 98-8 fish taken at Fripp Island by J. Darriano in June of 1981. Other big amberjack taken in the Carolinas were a 73-0 fish at the Ocean City Pier, 63-0 and 55-0 fish at the Jolly Roger Pier, and a 61-8 fish also caught by Jack Long. Fish from 40 to 50 pounds have been caught at the Surf City, Outer Banks, and Nags Head piers. Fish in the thirties are taken everywhere.

often enough to provide lots of excitement.

Winston-Salem angler Jack Long was on the Triple S Pier in Atlantic Beach rigged up for king mackerel with a big 6/0 Penn reel packed with 900 yards of 30-pound-test line. He was watching his live bluefish bait when three big heads came up out of the gloom. The smallest one got his bluefish. After just about stripping the line off the 6/0 reel, the fish was finally brought under control, and Jack, who has caught plenty of big amberjack before, was astounded by his catch, which tipped the scales (after he found

Amberjack are caught on king mackerel rigs, hitting live bluefish, mullet, menhaden, thread herring, or anything else that moves. They don't cut off the rear of the bait like king mackerel but inhale it like cobia and tarpon. Hooking them is no problem, but landing them is a different matter. Extremely strong and great runners, the largest jacks require heavy tackle.

The only similar jack in our area, although rare inshore, is the almaco jack (*Seriola rivoliana*), which has seven spines in its dorsal fin vs. eight spines in the amberjack.

Small jacks are abundant around the southern piers in summer and are often taken on cut bait. They are white-meated and sweeter than big jacks. Larger fish are edible but seldom eaten because the flesh is usually infested with unsightly larval tapeworms. The worms are harmless.

CREVALLE JACK

Fishermen call this fish the "Jack Crevalle," as though it were named for a person. It wasn't. Jacks are a family of fishes, and there are many kinds, such as bar jack, horse-eye jack, almaco jack, and—in this case—crevalle jack. Easily distinguished from the amberjack by its markings, blunt head, and forward-weighted body, the crevalle jack (*Caranx hippos*) is a powerful fighter that gets big enough to challenge any tackle. Ranging northward to Massachusetts, small ones are commonly caught from ocean piers, bridges, and jetties, big ones less often. Many crevalle jacks are taken on cut bait and small lures. Fish from 34 to over 40 pounds have been caught on king mackerel rigs at the Jolly Roger, Yaupon, Nags Head, and Barnacle Bill piers. The state records are 41-8 for North Carolina and 37-2 for South Carolina. The largest crevalle jack on record was 55 pounds, and an unidentified jack of 70 pounds may have been this species.

Schools of crevalle jacks will invade estuaries, running up into fresh water. This love of low

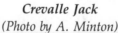

Crevalle Jack
(Photo by A. Minton)

93

salinities subjects them to fish kills when exposed to sudden temperature changes in northern coastal rivers or southern power plant discharge canals. These kills may involve thousands of 5- to 20-pounders over a mile or more of river.

TARPON

The biggest tarpon on record was a Lake Maracaibo, Venezuela, horse weighing 283 pounds. But we get big specimens of *Megalops atlanticus* in the Carolinas also, and any angler who thinks he has to go to Florida or South America for the silver king just doesn't know what we have in our own backyard.

From July to September, vast schools of perhaps two thousand big tarpon are sighted near Hatteras Inlet and off Bald Head Island. You can bet that other sightings occur but are kept secret. Few of these schooling fish will take a hook, but when the herd breaks up into small packs, the fish begin to feed. They will hit dead spot or croaker on the bottom of the oceanfront shoals near the capes or inside the sounds, live pinfish suspended from a balloon anywhere, or live bluefish on King mackerel rigs from piers.

Just about all Carolina fish are over 40 pounds. Some of our top fish were 164-0 (Indian Beach Pier), 159-0 (Paradise Pier), 152-0 (Crystal Pier), 142-0 (Emerald

(Courtesy of Charles Moore, South Carolina Marine Resources)

Isle Pier), 124-8 (Paradise Pier), 128-0 (Surfside Pier), 118-0, 110-0 (Dolphin Pier), 94-0 (Morehead and Frisco piers), 86-0 (Surf City Pier), 81-0 (Iron Steamer Pier), and many in the 70s and 60s throughout our area.

John Freeman's 164-pounder took a live bluefish and just about stripped all 600 yards of 30-pound-test dacron line from his Penn 4/0. That's light tackle for tarpon, which have a habit of greyhounding toward Portugal when hooked on an ocean pier. So the next time you see a television show with somebody in a silly hat taking one on a fly rod, remember that his reel probably holds at least 500 yards of heavy backing and the water body is an estuary, lake, or river where the fish can't run far enough to strip the reel.

Tarpon are heat-loving inshore fish that look like huge herrings. They enter the open ocean to spawn, and the larvae swim back into the coastal marshes. These "glass eel" or leptocephalus larvae look like larval eels but have fishlike tails just like their close relatives, the bonefish and lady-fish.

Tarpon occur throughout Pamlico Sound and at the mouth of the Pamlico River, and are sometimes trapped in gill nets. (They also occur in Virginia waters.)

SHARKS

It was early one July night, and Buz Boetticher was rowing the big shark baits out for the entire group. Some three hundred yards from the pier, he was surrounded by a silvery school of menhaden, which glistened on the surface of the moonlit water. As he passed through the school, there was a sharp scraping noise, and the raft was bumped, rubbed, and lifted from below. Buz's heart was still pounding after whatever it was had moved off. He continued rowing the last bait out another hundred yards, eased it over the side, and rowed back as fast as his aching limbs would allow.

About an hour later, it was Buz's ratchet that screamed into

575 lb. Dusky Shark
Caught from Jennette's Pier by Buzz Boetticher (Photo by Mike Williams)

the night, as an unseen shark carried off the fish head. It was to be a battle. When it was done, Buz had beached a 575-pound dusky shark. His only thought: had they met earlier that night, out in the school of menhaden?

It wasn't too many years ago that sharks were ignored or disdained by sportsmen, deprecatingly called "old garbage mouths," maulers of marlin, destroyers of beautiful game fish

95

meant to be records or mounts, and unworthy of any fishing efforts except lethal ones based on some vaguely imagined vengeance. Charter skippers complained of sharks on the billfish grounds, and "only a shark" described a day of failure. Only after the reality of a fight with a greyhounding mako or a horrendous hammerhead would sportsmen dare to suggest that sharks could, in fact, be just as exciting as any other game fish. Eventually, the International Game Fish Association recognized the mako as a sport fish, and other species were to follow. Today, IGFA recognizes the great white (known as the white pointer in Australia), mako, porbeagle, tiger (but not the sand tiger), blue, thresher, and hammerhead sharks as game fish. Other species will follow as anglers develop the skills to tell one shark from another. Advertisements in sportsmen's magazines for charter trips today offer not only tuna and billfish, but also sharks. Less than twenty years ago, that was unheard of. Only Captain Frank Mundus and his charter boat, *Cricket II*, out of Cove Marina in Montauk, New York, with his ads for "monster fishing," would sail after these unwanted and unappreciated nuisances. But Mundus was a loner, a man who killed pilot whales for shark chum, and his activities were anathema to other charter skippers. It was Mundus, in fact, who was the model for the fictional shark-hating skipper in the motion picture *Jaws*.

But what the movies did for popularizing shark hunting, television did for romanticizing the beauty of sharks. In a one-two punch, the public was exposed to a love-hate affair with sharks and sharking, and it was inevitable that tagging, which combined the hunt with live release, would be the direction taken by today's sportsmen.

That direction was encouraged by Jack Casey, Director of the Cooperative Shark Tagging Program headquartered at the National Marine Fisheries Service Laboratory at Narragansett, Rhode Island. Every season, Jack travels the tournament circuit from Rhode Island to Virginia to promote tagging, to provide expert identification in cases of doubt, to conduct or oversee necropsies, and to encourage the study and live release of sharks in order to learn more about their migrations, growth rates, feeding habits, population sizes, and fecundity. His boundless energies have stimulated the sport of sharking and promoted the growth of shark clubs. Today, there are shark clubs all along the Atlantic coast and tournaments all season. In our area, the main clubs are the Charleston Shark Club and the Virginia Beach Sharkers (who do a lot of their fishing in North Carolina waters).

The Virginia Beach Sharkers are typical of today's shark clubs. Releases are encouraged, and the fifty to sixty active men and women have all taken tests to become certified taggers under the NMFS Cooperative Shark Tagging Program. Upon passing the test for identifying sharks, members are invited to participate in the tagging program, given a supply of tags and instructions for inserting them, data cards for information on each shark, and a patch which each wears with well-deserved pride. Only trophy sharks or sharks carrying tags are kept.

Not all clubs, of course, promote releases. Some go for the largest sharks they can land, taking the jaws as trophies and the meat as food.

Most sharks, especially the smaller individuals, are among the finest of seafoods when first cut into small cubes or slabs and then presoaked for two hours in a weakly acidic solution of water with vinegar, orange, lemon, grapefruit, or lime juice. Presoaking a fresh shark steak in a vinegar and oil or herbal Italian dressing prior to grilling over charcoal will make any non-believer a shark meat addict. It has

taken years for anglers to learn that soaking shark in salted water does nothing except make it salty!

Today sharking is everyman's sport, if he can afford reels larger than 4/0, a gimbal rod belt, and a Florida shoulder harness.

While most sharking is done from boats, a good deal is done from piers, jetties, and beaches, where a sharker can dig his feet into something solid and lean his back into the battle. Sharks are best fought sitting down, and beach sharkers often have a legless fighting chair fitted with a gimbal for the rod butt. At Cape Hatteras, a couple of the regulars have bolted a standard big game fighting chair onto the bed of their pickup truck, which is backed down close to the berm.

It's a sport for a group of at least two or three people, for help is always needed in landing these big fish. It is no game for people who fool around or underestimate the power and dangers involved with handling such strong creatures. The last thing sharking is, is "fun," any more than bringing down a bear is "fun." It's serious business.

Most of today's sharkers are adept at telling one shark from another and never use the meaningless term, "sand shark." Most can spot a sand tiger at a glance by its gangly teeth, a tiger by its stripes or blotches, and a lemon by its equal-sized dorsal fins, and can distinguish among the species of hammerheads.

It's no longer as difficult as it seems. Several publications, written specifically for shark anglers, are now available and they range in price from cheap to free. These include *Angler's Guide to Sharks of the Northeastern United States* (U.S. Fish & Wildlife Service Circular 179, Superintendent of Documents, Washington, D.C. 20402); *Sharks, Sawfish, Skates and Rays of the Carolinas,* (F. J. Schwartz, 3407 Arendell Street, Morehead City, N.C. 28577); *An Angler's Guide to South Carolina Sharks* (Marine Resources Department, Box 12559, Charleston, S.C. 29412); and *The Sharks of North American Waters* (Drawer C, Texas A&M University Press, College Station, Tex. 77843).

There are shark clubs in our area that fish the North and South Carolina beaches and piers. For more information on sharking, write to the Virginia Beach Sharkers, P.O. Box 12025, Norfolk, Va. 23502, or the Greater Charleston Shark Club, P.O. Box 32171, Charleston, S.C. 29407. For information on the Cooperative Tagging Program, get in touch with Jack Casey, NOAA-NMFS, Northeast Fisheries Center, Narragansett, R.I. 02882.

Rigging terminal tackle for sharking from shore is quite different from offshore fishing. Because you cannot chase the fish, you need a lot of line capacity. Anything over 4/0 will provide some sport, and novices tend to invest in a 6/0. The serious sharker uses 9/0 to 12/0 reels loaded with 80- to 130-pound-test dacron line.

Terminal tackle varies in different locations. Most depend on a two-hook rig to provide a good hook-up, and these might be in series or parallel. On Florida beaches, sharkers use a fixed 14/0 hook and a slider 12/0 to 14/0 hook within the terminal five-foot segment of heavy wire. This piece attaches to a center six-foot length of braided wire, which is joined through a barrel swivel to an inner six-foot length of braided wire. A heavy (up to a pound) lead pyramid sinker is tied to the barrel swivel.

On the middle Atlantic coast, the typical terminal rig is a wishbone arrangement of 600-pound-test cable with 10/0 to 16/0 fixed hooks and twenty feet of #15 wire leader. Sinkers are not used, the weight of the bait and tackle being sufficient to hold the rig in place.

Many sharkers use IGFA regulation terminal gear, so that they are not excluded from world record contention. Not me. I like a simple rig consisting of two large hooks in series, bolted to a five-foot length of light chain. The chain is connected to a fifteen-foot length of cable, of the type used to crank small boats onto trailers. Chain, cable, and connectors are inexpensively purchased at K-Mart or some other discount store. More expensive, and lighter, cable is available at marinas. While the IGFA won't even consider sharks caught this way, I don't know of a shark that can bite through a chain (lots of them bite through cable).

Getting the rig out depends on weather conditions and where you fish. Many sharks are taken straight down from a pier or bridge in as little as five feet of water. If a longshore or offshore

Conventional Reel for Shark Fishing

wind is blowing, you can get the bait well away from the pier's pilings or bridge's stanchions by adding a float. The most popular float is an inflated, large plastic trash bag that is lightly hooked or tied to the rig. After reaching the targeted distance, the bait can be maintained there, suspended from the float, or jerked hard to rip free from the float so that it will sink. A plastic milk jug is a good float. Surf fishermen may take the bait offshore in a small inflatable raft, in a jon boat, or even on a surfboard. Some Virginia anglers, like Buz Boetticher and his group, lower both a raft and one of their club members from the pier by means of a harness, but that requires considerable nerve and skill.

The best baits for sharking on the surface are a live bluefish or any other big fish that will set up struggling vibrations. For sharking on the bottom or at mid-depth, the preferred baits are chunks of stingray, skate, other shark, tuna or mackerel heads, side slabs, or any other kind of juicy or oily fish meat. All baits should be fresh or maintained on ice. Rotten fish, mammalian parts, and chicken blood are neither necessary nor as good as ordinary fresh fish. Sharks are predators, not buzzards.

Sharks can be identified with reasonable certainty by using a fishery biologist's "key." But it must be used correctly. You cannot just skip around for the characteristics that seem to describe your shark. A key is reliable only if you begin at the beginning and let it take you along step by step. The reason is that early steps take certain characteristics into account, and these choices are then included in the decisions further on down. So begin at the beginning, and you will identify your sharks correctly.

TABLE 2. KEY TO SOUTHERN INSHORE SHARKS

1a. Barbels on nostrils . . . . Nurse.
1b. No barbels on nostrils . . . . 2.
2a. Heavy spine in front of each dorsal fin . . . . Spiny Dogfish.
2b. Dorsal fins without spines . . . . 3.
3a. Pectoral fins expanded as in rays . . . . Angel Shark.
3b. Pectoral fins normally shaped . . . . 4.
4a. Head expanded and flattened . . . . 19.
4b. Head normally shaped . . . . 5.
5a. Upper lobe of tail about as long as body . . . . Thresher.
5b. Upper lobe of tail not especially long . . . . 6.
6a. Teeth protruding out of mouth when closed . . . . Sand Tiger.
6b. Teeth not visible when mouth closed . . . . 7.
7a. Both dorsal fins about equal in size . . . . 8.
7b. Front dorsal fin much larger than rear dorsal . . . . 10.
8a. Eyes almond-shaped, teeth tiny . . . . 9.
8b. Eyes round, teeth well developed . . . . Lemon.
9a. Lower lobe of tail pointing downward . . . . Smooth Dogfish.
9b. Lower lobe of tail pointing backward . . . . Florida Dogfish.
10a. Body distinctly blotched or striped . . . . Tiger.
10b. Body lightly marked or unmarked . . . . 11.
11a. Strong tail keel,* black blotch in armpit . . . . White.
11b. Weak or absent tail keel, no armpit blotch . . . . 12.
12a. Anal fin more forward than second dorsal . . . . Sharpnose.
12b. Anal fin even with or behind second dorsal . . . . 13.
13a. Distinct ridge on back between dorsal fins . . . . 14.
13b. No ridge on back between dorsal fins . . . . 15.
14a. Front of first dorsal in front of armpit . . . . Sandbar.
14b. Front of first dorsal over or behind armpit . . . . Dusky.
15a. Space between nostrils longer than space between
        front of mouth and tip of nose . . . . Bull.
15b. Space between nostrils shorter than space between
        front of mouth and tip of nose . . . . 16.
16a. Dark smudge or blotch under tip of nose . . . . Blacknose.
16b. No dark smudge under tip of nose . . . . 17.
17a. Fins with dark markings on tips . . . . 18.
17b. Fins without dark markings on tips . . . . Finetooth.

TABLE 2. KEY TO SOUTHERN INSHORE SHARKS—continued

18a. Width of eye less than a fifth the length
of the first gill slit . . . . Spinner.
18b. Width of eye more than a fifth the length
of the first gill slit . . . . Blacktip.
19a. Front margin of head broadly rounded . . . . Bonnethead.
19b. Front margin of head hammer-shaped . . . . 20.
20a. Front midpoint of head straight . . . . Smooth Hammerhead.
20b. Front midpoint of head slightly notched . . . . 21.
21a. Teeth saw-edged . . . . Great Hammerhead.
21b. Teeth smooth-edged . . . . 22.
22a. Fifth gill slit above pectorals . . . . Smalleye Hammerhead.
22b. Fifth gill slit behind pectorals . . . . Scalloped Hammerhead.

* The only other keeled sharks are makos, but only a single mako has been reported from the surf zone. A great white has serrated, triangular teeth, while the teeth of a mako are elongated and smooth-edged.

Notes on Species

Nurse shark (*Ginglymostoma cirratum*). Not a hard fighter, this small-toothed bottom shark reaches a length of about twelve feet and is most common to the south. Small ones have markings.

Sand tiger (*Odontaspis taurus*). Very common shallow-water, inshore sharks throughout our area, sand tigers are weak fighters distinguished by gangly teeth, markings on the body, all the gill slits in front of the pectoral fins, and both dorsal fins the same size. They average three to seven feet and 150 pounds. A 260-pounder was taken at Charleston. The jaws make nice trophies and the meat is excellent.

Thresher shark (*Alopias vulpinus*). Attains great length, and fifteen-footers are common. A 740-pounder was taken off New Zealand, but these world-wide sharks might be taken anywhere. Not common inshore. The bigeye thresher (*Alopias superciliosus*) never comes to the beach zone but is common offshore at Cape Hatteras from April through June. Its second dorsal is well in front of its anal. A 406-pound bigeye thresher was taken off Johns Island, S.C.

Great white (*Carcharodon carcharias*). Widely dispersed in the Mid-Atlantic Bight, whites also occur in our area. An unidentified shark ate a third of a big blue marlin off Morehead City in June, 1984. Three months later, commercial fishermen working fifty miles south of Beaufort Inlet caught and landed a 2,080-pound, fifteen-foot great white shark. A sixteen-footer that weighed 2,400 pounds was recently caught off New York. NMFS located a group of whites off New York City beaches recently but did not advertise the find, which went largely unrecorded. Whites are taken from jetties in Australia and penetrate into the surf zone in California. The largest recorded was twenty-one feet long (not weighed) from Cuba in 1945. White sharks have been observed feeding on dead whales and discarded big bluefish heads. Above Cape Cod and off the West Coast they eat seals and sea lions.

Blacknose (*Carcharhinus acronotus*). A small fish, usually less than five feet in length and more common to the south.

Dusky shark (*Carcharhinus obscurus*). Very common in our area, with fish up to eleven feet taken. A 467-pounder was caught at Charleston and a 610-pounder at Nags Head.

Sandbar shark (*Carcharhinus plumbeus*). Also known as New York ground shark and brown shark, this very common species enters estuaries and also occurs in the Gulf Stream. One tagged individual covered the two thousand miles between New England and Mexico. The sandbar shark feeds most actively between 1:30 and 4:30 a.m. and most frequently on blue crabs and menhaden. It lives at least twenty to thirty years but attains a length of only about eight feet. A 154-pounder was taken in South Carolina.

Bull shark (*Carcharhinus leucas*). Abundant in the Gulf of

489 lb. Dusky Shark
Caught by David Wolfe at Nags Head, North Carolina
(Photo by Mike Williams)

Mexico, this big inshore bottom shark is the same one that occurs landlocked in Lake Nicaragua. It feeds mostly on stingrays, sandbar sharks, and fish and probably attains 500 pounds in weight. A 409-pounder was taken at Charleston. This is considered a dangerous shark because it runs into rivers, attains great size, and is aggressive.

Blacktip shark (*Carcharhinus limbatus*). Not a large shark, it occurs inshore only during the warm months and is abundant

102

off our beaches during the summer. The white anal fin is a good identifying characteristic. It has been known to leap out of the water like a spinner shark. A 133-pounder is the South Carolina state record.

Spinner shark (*Carcharhinus brevipinna*). Most common below the Carolina capes, this small to medium-sized shark is a spectacular fighter that is often seen leaping clear of the water.

Finetooth shark (*Carcharhinus isodon*). This shallow-water shark is common in South Carolina waters during the late summer. It enters the surf zone, where it feeds during daylight hours on small fish.

Longfinned mako (*Isurus paucus*). A single report from beach sharkers in Florida prompts inclusion of this oceanic shark here. The Florida fish was foul-hooked, broke free, and died of its wounds.

Tiger shark (*Galeocerdo cuvieri*). The largest meat-eating sharks of the Atlantic coast and the largest that come into shallow water, tigers are a lot more common than most anglers (and swimmers) realize. Thousand-pounders have been taken from just about every Atlantic coast state. The Virginia Beach Sharkers have taken a few from their coastal waters. In the Carolinas, Walter Maxwell took a 1,150-pounder from the pier at Yaupon Beach, the world record

1,780-pounder from the Cherry Grove Pier at North Myrtle Beach, and lost one the day before his record that was much larger. And he does it all with IGFA regulation tackle (no chains). Tigers eat anything, including sea turtles, sea birds, and whelks. They are not predatory man-eaters but will scavenge drifting, dead bodies. One fish tagged off New York traveled 1,850 miles to Costa Rica.

Smooth dogfish (*Mustelus canis*). This abundant dogfish doesn't get very large and is usually considered a nuisance. It is edible.

Florida dogfish (*Mustelus norrisi*). Very similar to and a lot rarer than the smooth dogfish, it occurs north to South Carolina.

Lemon shark (*Negaprion brevirostris*). One of our more abundant large, inshore sharks, the lemon is distinguished by its equal-sized dorsal fins and lack of markings. It is potentially dangerous to swimmers. A 317-pounder was taken at Charleston and a 421-pounder at Kure Beach.

Sharpnose shark (*Rhizoprionodon terraenovae*). This is a tiny shark, attaining only about three feet in length and ten pounds in weight. Very sleek and pretty, it usually has a white rear margin to the pectoral fins.

Bonnethead shark (*Sphyrna tiburo*). Also called the shovelnose shark, this smallest member of the hammerhead group is abundant in the Gulf of Mexico and uncommon in our area. Most are about the size of small dogfish.

Smalleye hammerhead (*Sphyrna tudes*). A tropical hammerhead, the smalleye is known from the Gulf of Mexico but has not yet been reported from our waters.

Smooth hammerhead (*Sphyrna zygaena*). This is a common hammerhead to the north, frequently found in our area. Attaining thirteen feet in length, it is a dangerous shark. The smooth, great, and scalloped hammerheads all occur in our waters, but state record keepers generally don't distinguish among the species. A 473-pound unidentified hammerhead, probably this species, was taken at Edisto Island and a 710-pounder at Nags Head.

Great hammerhead (*Sphyrna mokarran*). This southern hammerhead occurs from the Gulf of Mexico to the Carolinas and attains a length of twenty feet. Common in oceanic waters, it also frequents our beaches. A very powerful shark, it is seldom landed.

Scalloped hammerhead (*Sphyrna lewini*). A common hammerhead in Carolina waters, this moderately sized fish is usually found offshore but enters our beach areas during colder months.

Spiny dogfish (*Squalus acanthias*). This abundant, edible shark is most often seen during the cold months. It attains about five feet in length, and three-footers are common. Ranging both sides of the Atlantic, this was the "fish" in "fish and chips" before stocks were depleted and the British switched to plaice (flounder).

Angel shark (*Squatina dumerili*). The angelfish or sand devil is also called monkfish, but that name is also used for an unrelated, edible angler fish. Nobody eats angel sharks, as they are thin and provide too little meat. They are sometimes taken on light tackle by flounder fishermen. Angel sharks average less than thirty pounds and get up to about five feet in length. While the teeth are small (less than a half-inch long in average fish) and not significant, the jaws are powerful and these fish bite!

SKATES, RAYS, AND SAWFISH

The elasmobranch fishes are broadly divided into the sharks and rays. Sharks have gill slits and spiracles (holes) on the sides of the head, but rays (which include the skates and sawfishes) have their gill slits below and spiracles above. Rays split off from sharks early in their evolution and adapted to life on the bottom. Some, like mantas, have changed again.

The different groups of rays have certain characteristics in common. For example, skates (genus *Raja*) have no stingers but possess a thick, prickly tail. Almost all the other rays have stingers. (To release any stingray, face toward the front of the fish so that the tail points away from you. Then lift the fish by inserting your fingers in the spiracles. Although the tail can whip around and hit you, the stingers are at the base and the tail tip is harmless.)

Skates have small dorsal fins. The dorsal fins of the rays are completely absent or reduced to a low membrane or ridge of skin. Most skates have prickly skin, while most rays have smooth skin.

Certain larger skates have been used as scallop substitutes in years past, and all skates are edible. Rays have rarely been eaten in the past, but Virginia Sea Grant is promoting the consumption of cownose rays.

Some rays have electric organs, something not found in any other elasmobranchs but which occur in a few kinds of bony fishes.

Sawfishes are the only elasmobranchs that have developed teeth on the outside of an elongated snout. The sawfishes are large animals that penetrate well up into fresh water. They are edible but little used as food in this country.

I have constructed a simple key to the identification of southern inshore rays but, as with the sharks, you must begin at the beginning and proceed one couplet at a time to end up with the correct answer.

TABLE 3. KEY TO SOUTHERN INSHORE RAYS

1a. Gill slits located on the sides . . . . sharks (p.95)
1b. Gill slits located below . . . . 2.
2a. Snout long and flat with external side teeth . . . . 3.
2b. Snout not long, not flat, not externally toothed . . . . 4.
3a. Twenty or fewer teeth on each side of snout . . . . . Largetooth sawfish.
3b. Twenty-five teeth or more on each side
    of snout . . . . Smalltooth sawfish.
4a. Stingers absent . . . . 5.
4b. Stingers present . . . . 9.
5a. Tail fin present . . . . 6.
5b. Tail fin absent . . . . 8.
6a. Disc longer than wide . . . . Guitarfish.
6b. Disc not longer than wide . . . . 7.
7a. Disc rounded in front . . . . Electric Ray.
7b. Disc straight in front . . . . Torpedo.

TABLE 3. KEY TO SOUTHERN INSHORE RAYS—continued

8a. Tail very prickly, about as long as body........................ 14.
8b. Tail smooth, shorter than body.............. Smooth Butterfly Ray.
9a. Tail thin and whiplike .... 10.
9b. Tail thick and clublike............................ Yellow Stingray.
10a. Tail much shorter than body.................. Spiny Butterfly Ray.
10b. Tail at least as long as body .... 11.
11a. Midline of snout deeply indented .... Cownose Ray.
11b. Midline of snout protruding or rounded....................... 12.
12a. Upper body with many white spots .... Eagle Ray.
12b. Upper body without white spots .... 13.
13a. Snout strongly protruding.......................... Bullnose Ray.
13b. Snout rounded or angled, not strongly protruding .... 17.
14a. Underside with distinct black
     spots or lines .... Florida Barndoor Skate.
14b. Underside white or with gray smudges........................ 15.
15a. Upper wings with eyespot markings.................. Winter Skate.
15b. Upper wings without eyespot markings .... 16.
16a. At least one thorn between fins on tail............. Clearnose Skate.
16b. No thorns between fins on tail .... Little Skate.
17a. Tail without a ridge or finfold.................. Roughtail Stingray.
17b. Tail with a ridge or finfold .... 18.
18a. Snout smoothly even.......................... Southern Stingray.
18b. Snout slightly projecting....................................... 19.
19a. Distance between spiracles shorter than distance
     between eye and snout .... Atlantic Stingray.
19b. Distance between spiracles longer than distance
     between eye and snout .... Bluntnose Stingray.

Notes on Species

Smalltooth sawfish (*Pristis pectinata*). The only sawfish likely to occur in our waters, ranging from South America northward to Chesapeake Bay. It attains a size of eighteen feet and a thousand pounds.

Largetooth sawfish (*P. perotteti*). This sawfish gets a little bigger than the smalltooth and is more common in Florida and Texas waters. Both species enter shallow water, attacking schools of fish by slashing with their snout and then returning to pick up the pieces. Sawfish are powerful fish that readily take cut bait. The toothed snout makes a nice trophy, and the meat is of high quality.

Atlantic guitarfish (*Rhinobatos lentiginosus*). Guitarfish look a bit like angel sharks, but the gill slits are on the bottom. The average guitarfish is two feet long and weighs thirty pounds, but they get about a foot longer. Ranging from Mexico to the Carolinas, they are common

Electric Ray

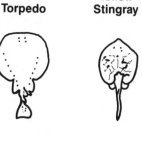

Torpedo

Yellow Stingray

Atlantic Stingray

Roughtail Stingray

Butterfly Ray

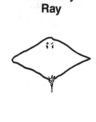

Skate

Angel Shark

Guitarfish

Sawfish

Spotted Eagle Ray

Bullnose Ray

Cownose Ray

here in the spring. These weak fighters are usually unhooked and returned to the water.

Lesser electric ray (*Narcine brasiliensis*). This ray is usually about a foot long, and round, with complex markings on a yellow to dark brown top. From Brazil to the Carolinas, this shallow-water summertime ray eats mostly sea worms. Although small, it can shock you out of your shorts. The best way to identify an electric ray is to grab it. If in doubt, cut the leader and drop the fish back into the briny.

Torpedo (*Torpedo nobiliana*). The torpedo is a giant electric ray well known in New England, where it invades pound nets to feed on trapped fish. Rare in our area, this black ray has a short, thick tail with a well-developed tail fin. It attains six feet and one hundred fifty pounds. The entire muscle mass is an electric generator. I saw one fellow's hair literally stand straight up when he grabbed the tail of a fifty-pounder and learned why the other fellows were all wearing rubber gloves.

Spiny butterfly ray (*Gymnura altavela*). The spiny butterfly ray is not often seen by sport fishermen; I have seen but three in twelve years, all on the same day in the same place. A large school was reported in North Carolina in 1914. Butterfly rays are much wider than long, attaining a wing span of thirteen feet. Their very short tails are armed with one or more stingers at the base.

Smooth butterfly ray (*Gymnura micrura*). Probably never attaining four feet across, this little ray ranges from Chesapeake Bay to the Gulf Coast, sometimes in great schools. It has no stingers.

Cownose ray (*Rhinoptera bonasus*). Locally called "mantas" because of the indented snout, these big, brown rays are abundant in Carolina waters. Real mantas are oceanic midwater plankton feeders, while cownose rays use powerful crushing plates in their jaws to feed on inshore shellfish. As they plow the bottom in small groups, they may be trailed by cobia picking up fish and crabs disturbed by the commotion. Cownose rays get up to four feet across and are excellent barbecued or smoked. They readily take a baited hook, although many are accidentally snagged. One or more stingers occur at the base of the tail.

Spotted eagle ray (*Aetobatus narinari*). This beautiful ray is polka dotted with white spots on its dark brown upper surface and white as snow beneath. Like manta rays, eagle rays sometimes leap clear of the water—an impressive sight in a fish that may be seven feet across and weigh a quarter of a ton. It ranges north to Chesapeake Bay, becoming progressively more common in inshore waters southward. Like the cownose, it has stingers and crushing jaw plates and may take a baited hook. Only the small ones are usually landed, the larger ones manageable only with shark tackle.

Bullnose ray (*Myliobatis freminvillei*). The bullnose ray is rare on our coast. Averaging two feet across but attaining three, it is dark above without markings and white below. It has a protruding snout like a spotted eagle ray but is colored like a cownose ray. It has impressive stingers and should be handled with caution.

Yellow stingray (*Urolophus jamaicensis*). This rounded ray is uncommon north of Florida but does occur in shallow waters of both Carolinas, where it feeds on shrimp, crabs, worms, and small fish. It has a thick tail ending in a fishlike tail fin, like an electric ray or torpedo. There the similarity ends, for this one has stingers. The yellowish back is decorated with a netlike pattern, quite unlike any other ray. Top size is about two feet long and a foot wide.

Roughtail stingray (*Dasyatis centroura*). Probably the largest of the world's stingrays, the roughtail is characterized by a prickly disc and sometimes a prickly tail. One on record was seven feet wide and fourteen feet long. Abundant around Cape Cod, it becomes rare south of Chesapeake Bay.

Southern (*Dasyatis americana*), **Atlantic** (*D. sabina*), **and bluntnose** (*D. sayi*) **stingrays.** These abundant, brownish-black rays average one to two feet across. They have one or more stingers at the base of the tail and have caused grief to people wading barefoot in the shallows. These small stingrays are not used as food, but they make excellent shark bait.

Florida barndoor skate (*Raja floridana*). A newly recognized species that occurs in Florida and the Carolinas, this skate reaches five feet and forty pounds, eats all sorts of shellfish and fish, including small sharks, and is the only big skate with tiny black lines and spots underneath. In years past, the wings of northern barndoors (and perhaps the Florida fish) were cut and sold as scallops.

Clearnosed skate (*Raja eglanteria*). The clearnosed skate is the only abundant skate on the Carolina coast. It eats anything, lives up to five years, and attains a length of about two feet. Great migrations of clearnosed skates often result in a fisherman catching forty in a day. During these migrations it is almost impossible to hook any other kind of bottom fish. These migrations are unisexual, the males and females making separate trips. The brown "mermaid's purses" seen on the beaches are egg cases of skates. Edible but seldom used as food, whole clearnosed skates make excellent shark bait, while belly strips are good for flounder.

Little (*Raja erinacea*) **and winter** *(R. ocellata)* **skates.** These other skates are not common on our coast, occurring mostly to the north.

Skinned skate and ray wings are good to eat. The French method is to cook them for five to ten minutes in a mixture of one part vinegar to five parts water with a level teaspoon of salt per quart of liquid. While they're cooking, take a small pan and heat a half cup of butter until it turns brown. Don't worry about the smoke. Stir in a quarter cup of red wine vinegar and a heaping tablespoon of capers, and cook for another minute. Remove the skate wings, dry them with paper towels, and pour the butter sauce over them. You've just prepared Raie Beurre Noir.

RED DRUM

Nothing could be finer than to fish in Carolina for big red drum. When brisk mid-October winds drive the copper-plated giants out of their summer foraging grounds within North Carolina's Pamlico Sound and onto the ocean beaches of the northern Outer Banks, knowledgeable saltwater fishermen from all over the United States begin their fall migration to Hatteras, Portsmouth, and Ocracoke islands. Some 80% of all North Carolina citation red drum are taken during October and November from the waters of these islands.

But, while outdoor writers are joining the hordes of fishermen working the beaches, many of the regulars who know these fish are up on the piers of Hatteras Island, where the greatest numbers of big red drum are invariably caught.

Although no state can compare with North Carolina, South Carolina and Virginia also get some big drum. The South Carolina state record red drum is a 75-pounder taken at Murrells Inlet in 1965. But big reds are uncommon in the Palmetto State, which is better known for its abundant spottail bass or small red drum. The best big drum locations here are Murrells and Fripp inlets.

An 85-pound red drum was taken in Virginia in 1981. This sister state to our north at one time held the all-tackle world record. I believe that the Virginia giants are members of the Pamlico Sound population that have foraged northward, but the tagging data do not yet show any clear pattern.

Until 1984, the IGFA all-tackle world record was Elvin Hooper's 90-pounder taken from the Hatteras Island Pier at Rodanthe on November 7, 1973. Then on November 7, 1984, David Deuel, a scientist with the National Marine Fisheries Service and an expert on red drum, smashed

110

that record with a 94-pounder from the surf near Avon. That monster was taken just at the end of the most spectacular beach and pier run of big red drum in Hatteras Island's recorded history. During a three-day period, more than one hundred forty drum from thirty-seven to sixty-one pounds were decked on the Hatteras Island Pier alone.

Pier fishing for big red drum is an Outer Banks specialty. Enormous pendulum casts are made to those rare but well-known breaks in the outer bar that lead off the beach and into deep water. Those breaks, or rips, are channels for outrushing slough water carrying baitfish to waiting packs of big drum. If you can't find the breaks, you won't find the concentrations of fish that lie in wait just at the edge of deep water.

You won't see many spinning outfits in use on these piers, where long-distance casting skill makes all the difference. The standard tackle is a stiff, heavy, ten-foot conventional rod, the "Hatteras heaver," loaded with seventeen- to twenty-five-pound-test monofilament line. A long shock leader takes the force of the cast. Pier fishermen use the same rigs and baits as beach fishermen.

Even more often than on the beach, a big red drum is likely to swim shoreward with the bait, so that the first indication of a

fish is the line rapidly going slack. Anglers who close their eyes and await the sound of a ratchet miss a lot of fish, as do people who wander around the pier. Those who catch the most fish never take their eyes from the lines.

Red drum are very strong, and the fight will be prolonged on even heavy tackle. Almost every fish is landed with a pier net so that it can be released alive. Some anglers drop the fish back into the water, but this can cause

Red Drum
Caught from Hatteras Island Pier, Rodanthe (Photo by Aycock Brown)

mortal internal damage. Any heavy fish should be gently lowered back into the water, the net then sloshed up and down until the fish swims free.

Small red drum (puppy drum, spottail bass) are taken earlier and in greater numbers. They often precede the appearance of big reds by about a month. Small reds travel in schools of similar-sized fish and frequently invade much shallower waters than their giant aunts and uncles. Many are taken by flounder fishermen on finger mullet, killifish, or strips of squid. Like big fish, however, they prefer the walls of sloughs and channels between bars.

Little reds are excellent gourmet fare. Their numbers are currently high and getting better because of a good spawning year in 1981, and perhaps 1982, from North Carolina to Florida.

If you decide to keep your fish, be aware that, in North Carolina, the minimum keeper size is fourteen inches, and no angler may possess more than two red drum in excess of thirty-two inches. You can get a certificate of achievement in North Carolina for any drum at least forty pounds in weight or forty-six inches in length.

BLACK DRUM

The distribution of black drum (*Pogonias cromis*) is tied to hard bottoms rather than latitude. The greatest number of giants are caught from small boats in Delaware Bay, well north of our area, yet other centers of distribution occur at the jetties below the Outer Banks. Black drum are even caught on the beaches at Buxton, but those are unusual individuals, "lost" according to some of the locals! Ranging from New Jersey to the Texas Gulf Coast and beyond, black drum are often found alongside sheepshead under bridges, at jetties and inshore outcrops, and wherever hard structure occurs.

Spring is the peak period for black drum. In early spring, aircraft pilots have spotted huge schools of giants far off the beaches of the Outer Banks making their way northward to Virginia and the Delmarva Peninsula. Seldom do these fish venture inshore to the sandy beaches of North Carolina, and where they come from is still not known. Perhaps they are migrants that have overwintered off the coasts of South Carolina and Georgia.

The state records in our area are an 80-pounder from the Cape Fear River of North Carolina in 1984 and an 89-pounder from Port Royal Sound, South Carolina, in 1978. Two fish, each weighing 111 pounds, were taken from Cape Charles, Virginia, in 1973 and 1974, while the world record of just over 113 pounds was taken at Lewes,

Black Drum
(Photo courtesy of Carolyn Toughill)

ripe female up into the water column, leaving a cloud of eggs and milt in their wake. The eggs hatch in a day or two, and the larvae make their way inshore to mud-bottomed marshes. In the fall, the young-of-the-year drum leave the marshes in a massive offshore migration for the winter. They will return the next spring and by the end of their first year will have grown to eight inches long. They will attain a length of three feet by the time they are ten years old and may live to be more than thirty-five years old.

Fishing for black drum is not a beach activity, as the fish seldom come into sandy bottom areas. Jetties and bridges are the best places, followed by piers adjacent to hard bottoms. Black drum venture in close to structures, so long-distance casting is not necessary and may be counterproductive.

Heavy tackle is advisable for big black drum. A 7/0 hook tied to 60- to 100-pound monofilament leader on a three-way swivel, and a simple bank sinker, is the simplest and most effective rig. Fish-finder rigs are not used.

The favored baits are chunks of clam, whole softshell crab, and squid. Black drum eat mostly shellfish. Where red and black drum occur together, fishermen make "clamwiches" of fish, clam, and crab. Hardshell

Delaware, in 1975. Black drum in the 90- to 100-pound range are not unusual north of our area.

Black drum spawn in the Delaware and Chesapeake Bay areas in the spring when the water temperature reaches 61° to 65° F. One or more males accompany a crabs make good bait. Remove the claws and legs and insert the hook into one joint socket and out the body. Change bait frequently, as crabs leak the juices necessary to attract fish.

Black drum are nibblers and don't always run off with the bait. It's necessary to "feel" constantly for weight on the line by lifting gently. If resistance is met, the force is increased strongly. Do not yank back hard and fast, as the bait may be ripped from the fish's lips. Short, heavy jabs will bury the hook.

Small black drum, common at bridges and hard-bottom piers all season, are delicious. Big ones are uncommon in our area, almost impossible to dress out because of their giant scales, and have coarse meat frequently infested with larval shark tapeworms, which appear as white cysts in the musculature. Many big drum are killed and left on the dock to rot north of our region. As a result, their numbers are way down. Carolina anglers are urged to release all big black drum.

BLUEFISH

While big bluefish are premier game fish from the surf, they are more readily taken from bridges, jetties, and piers that extend out over deeper water. The big chopper blues in the fifteen- to twenty-five-pound range are fish

of the cold months in the Carolinas. The best times are around December and April and any time in midwinter when warm winds are blowing onshore. The best locations are the capes and northward, although they might show up anywhere. Most pier and bridge anglers use cut mullet on Fireball rigs armed with heavy wire leaders. When the fish arrive in force, often heralded by wheeling gulls, anglers switch to Hopkins squids or other heavy metal cast-

Bluefish caught on Fireball rig.

ing lures. The hard strike of a bluefish as it stops a high-speed lure cold is one of the great thrills of shore fishing in the Carolinas. Fall and winter fish are always fat and hard-fighting, while some of the spring-run fish are thin and weak.

Fast and repetitive lure casting requires a backlash-proof system, and lots of casts in a hurry (when the birds are close) are more important than being able to throw big payloads. For these reasons, heavy spinning tackle is the favorite gear for big bluefish in the Carolinas.

Pier- and bridge-caught blues are gaffed. Pier gaffs have, on many occasions, retrieved entire fishing outfits that were leaning against a railing unattended, to be suddenly yanked overboard by a powerful bluefish. If spinning gear is used, set the drag loosely. For conventional tackle, it is sufficient to leave the reel in free-spool with the ratchet engaged.

LITTLE TUNNY

Locally called bonito, false albacore, or "Fat Albert," the little tunny (*Euthynnus alletteratus*) is a member of the mackerel and tuna family (Scombridae). It is distinguished from other small tunas by its pattern of branching stripes above the midline. The Atlantic bonito (*Sarda sarda*) has unbranched stripes above the midline, while the skipjack tuna (*Katsu-*

wonus pelamis) has unbranched stripes below the midline.

Wide-ranging throughout the Atlantic, the little tunny is an offshore fish north of our area, yet is caught in the surf here in the Carolinas. One reason is the high quality of our water.

Little tunny remain offshore during the warm months but hit our beaches in the fall and spring. A few are often mixed in with schools of giant bluefish. At other times, small pods of less than a dozen fish cruise just under the surface from shore to three or four miles out, where they are commonly seen attacking baitfish on the surface. Little tunny can be distinguished from bluefish in three ways. First, the birds overhead (if any) will be small groups of little terns rather than big groups of gulls. Second, you can see them breaking the water surface as they feed. And third, they usually occur in small groups rather than hordes covering over an acre. You may see one to three packs at a time from the vantage point of a pier. Sometimes, especially just before dark in early winter, the entire ocean will erupt with thousands of them. And they can disappear within minutes, leaving you wondering if you really saw them after all.

Little tunny will sometimes hit big Hopkins squids thrown for bluefish but are more likely to be caught on very small, silvery metal jigs. Favored lures are the Conner Z1H and the very smallest Hopkins Shorty. Because of their tendency to feed on tiny, silvery anchovies, the lure should be as small as possible. When little tunny are abundant, they'll readily take a live spot fished under a float or freelined out from the pier. Surprisingly, tiny baits are not required.

Average size is about four to eight pounds, but they get larger. The state records for "albacore" are a 25-pounder taken from Cape Lookout, North Carolina, and a 37-pounder from Charleston, South Carolina. Those may be misidentifications representing several other kinds of tunas, including the real albacore (*Thunnus alalunga*). The IGFA all-tackle world record little tunny was a 27-pounder taken from Key Largo, Florida.

Little tunny have red meat that turns dark tan when cooked. Most fishermen either use them for bait or release them alive. They make excellent strip baits for offshore trolling and can also be used as bait for cobia, bluefish, and sharks.

Raw, they are not very fishy tasting and are valued by Oriental gourmets for sashimi. To prepare sashimi, you will need to shop at an Oriental grocery for soy sauce and a tin of Japanese powdered horseradish. Ice and bleed the fish as soon as it is caught. Be careful to cut skinless fillets along, rather than across, the grain of the meat; it minimizes muscle damage and prolongs the fresh flavor. Store the fillets under ice until use. When ready to eat, take a teaspoon of the green powdered horseradish and mix with enough water to make a paste. Each person should receive a small dab of paste on the edge of a saucer of soy sauce. Serve bite-size pieces of tuna (and any other fresh, raw finfish or shellfish) on a bed of lettuce. Mix some paste in your soy sauce to taste; it's very piquant. Pick up a piece of fish, dredge it through the soy-paste mixture, and pop it in your mouth. I guarantee that you will never again use a little tunny for bait.

Little Tunny
Caught by Rich Szymanksi at Avon Pier

HOW TO KNOW THE SMALL INSHORE TUNAS

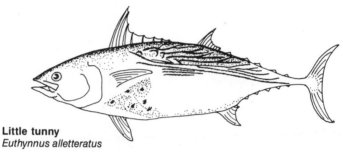

Little tunny
Euthynnus alletteratus

Branching lines above, smudges or spots below, abundant inshore.

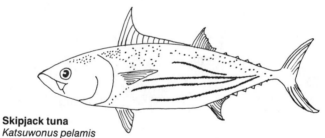

Skipjack tuna
Katsuwonus pelamis

Non-branching lines below, rare inshore.

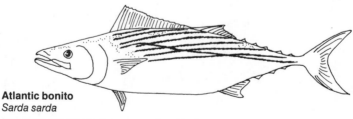

Atlantic bonito
Sarda sarda

Non-branching lines above, occasional inshore.

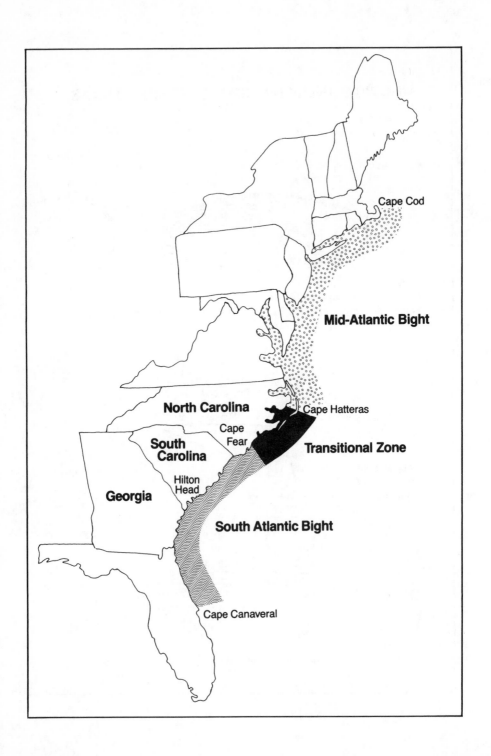

Cape Cod

Mid-Atlantic Bight

North Carolina

Cape Hatteras

Cape
Fear

South
Carolina

Transitional Zone

Hilton
Head

Georgia

South Atlantic Bight

Cape Canaveral

WHERE TO GO

The better places to fish along our coast are numerous, but so are the worse ones. Many is the time I've fished a location to no avail, only to learn later that I was just a hop, skip, and jump from some of the hottest action around. Knowing how to fish and when to go are important, but no less important is knowing the best places. It's also important to note that some places don't permit certain kinds of fishing, while others encourage them. Sharking, for example, is not allowed on Grand Strand piers, but you can do all you want farther south.

Piers and bridges are usually productive, but some are better than others at specific times of the year because they sit on a migratory route or are located close to an inlet, cape, or jetty. For example, bridges are great in late May because they attract big cobia; Outer Banks piers are good for big bluefish and red drum in spring and fall; and southern and central coastal piers are good for king mackerel during the summer and tarpon in the fall. Again, there are piers that don't allow king mackerel fishing, and your goal is to find a location where you can do what you want to do.

I have divided our coastline into three principal geographic zones that correspond to ocean basins, currents, and fish migrations. The first zone is the Mid-Atlantic Bight, which extends from Cape Cod to Cape Hatteras. Within the Mid-Atlantic Bight, I will describe the portion from Currituck Beach just south of the Virginia line to Cape Hatteras. My second zone will be called the Transition Zone and includes Cape Hatteras, Cape Lookout, and many of the beaches of the central coast of North Carolina. It is a transitional zone between the two bights of the Atlantic coast, and its fisheries vary from year to year, depending on winds, currents, and other natural phenomena. The third zone is the South Atlantic Bight, which begins with the Wilmington area and extends to Cape Canaveral. I will describe the portion from the Wilmington area, including Cape Fear, to Hilton Head.

THE MID-ATLANTIC BIGHT

The hot spots mapped and coded in this section were supplied by various local experts.

Locations marked with the prefix "T" were recommended by Damon Tatem of Tatem's Tackle Box in Nags Head. Locations marked with the prefix "J" were supplied by Ollie Jarvis of Dillon's Corner in Buxton.

T1. A stumpy area that can be reached by four-wheel drive, this beach location south of the Currituck Lighthouse is good in the fall for big bluefish during high tides. Striped bass are possible here in late fall and early winter. From June through October, flounder fishing is usually good. Because T1 is so far from any road, it's advisable to travel with another vehicle in case of stranding.

T2. The beach north of the Kitty Hawk Pier is a traditional area for spotted sea trout (specks). The peak period is September and October. It is often good in the spring, with April and May frequently providing fish for the few early surf casters.

Kitty Hawk Pier, Kitty Hawk, N.C. 27949, telephone (919) 261-2772. Located near the Currituck Sound Bridge, the pier is 714 feet long. The water depth is six to twenty-five feet, depending on the location of the shifting outer sand bar. Facilities include a tackle shop and restaurant. Motels and camping are nearby. The pier was built in 1953 and has been the site of several outstanding catches over the years, including a 57½-pound state rec-

ord striped bass and a previous all-tackle world record bluefish. Catches of channel bass, flounder, and big bluefish are especially good in April, May, October, and November. Big game fishing for kings is allowed at the end of the pier; the best times are around Mother's Day and again in the fall.

T3. Called the Old Station Area, this is an excellent steep beach that provides good surf casting from April through November.

Avalon Pier, Kill Devil Hills, N.C. 27948, telephone (919) 441-7494. Built in 1962, the Avalon Pier is 650 feet long, with a water depth at the end of roughly fifteen feet. There is a tackle shop and restaurant. Motels and campgrounds are nearby. The Avalon Pier provides good action for big bluefish and channel bass in April and May and again in October and November. During the summer it provides good fishing for spot, croaker, flounder, and whiting (sea mullet).

Nags Head Fishing Pier, Nags Head, N.C. 27959, telephone (919) 441-5141. The Nags Head Pier was built two years after the end of World War II. In 1957, it suffered the loss of 300 feet during a hurricane. Two years later another hurricane blew a wrecked ship through the middle of the pier. The infamous Ash Wednesday Storm of 1962, the worst storm ever to hit the

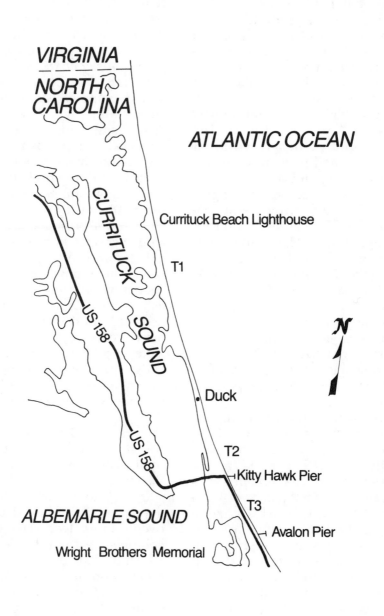

Outer Banks, completely destroyed it, but like so many other piers, it was rebuilt. Today, the pier is 740 feet long; there is a tackle shop, gift shop, restaurant, and cottages; and the current owners have facilities for campers. Fishing here is excellent for big bluefish and channel bass in April and May and late fall. Spot, croaker, whiting, flounder, and pompano action is good during much of the season. King mackerel fishing is best in early spring and late summer. Late fall sees good runs of little tunny. Many large game fish have been taken here, including a 35½-pound amberjack.

T4. Nags Head Water Tower, the Epstein Tract. This beach segment is easy to reach and provides good general fishing from April through November. Spring and fall surf casters often hit into big bluefish and gray sea trout.

Jennette's Ocean Pier and Motor Court, milepost 6.5, Nags Head, N.C. 27959, telephone (919) 441-6116. Located at the 6½-milepost marker in Nags Head, right at Whalebone Junction, where U.S. 64-264 meets the Outer Banks, Jennette's Pier is a lot more than just a landmark. This is the pier most used by Virginia and North Carolina sharkers on the northern Outer Banks. Any night during the summer or fall you might discover a shark club with their massive equipment and unusual skills, and if you ever want to start sharking, come here to watch how it's done. Bob Keller of Cleveland, Ohio, took a 610-pound dusky shark on this pier, following that up with a 720-pound hammerhead shark two years later. A model of the dusky hangs from the ceiling of the tackle shop. Many 150- to 200-pound sharks aren't even reported. The pier provides excellent fishing for flounder and gray sea trout much of the year, big blues in the spring and fall, and king mackerel in the spring. A 23½-pound little tunny was landed here, but at that time the species wasn't listed as a game fish by the IGFA. The pier was first built in 1939 and lasted for three years. By that time, we were into World War II and nobody was building fishing piers. Two years after the war's end, the pier was rebuilt but it was then extensively damaged by storms for three consecutive years during the 1950s and finally destroyed by the Ash Wednesday Storm. Today, it is 900 feet long, with the end depth varying from sixteen to twenty-three feet. The pier is equipped with a tackle shop, which has one of the largest reel repair shops in Virginia or North Carolina. The management also owns a thirty-five-unit motel (twenty-three with kitchens), and nine cottages. There are additional facilities throughout the area.

King Mackerel
Caught by Chuck Ellis at Outer Banks
Pier, South Nags Head (Photo by
Aycock Brown)

Outer Banks Pier, Nags Head, N.C. 27959, telephone (919) 441-5740. Located south of Whalebone Junction, the 650-foot-long pier is nestled in a residential area well removed from the hustle and bustle of Nags Head's motel and restaurant strip. The deepest part of this pier is not at the end but about fifty feet before, where the water is twenty-three to twenty-six feet deep. The end of the pier sits on a sandbar in ten to twelve feet of water. Facilities include a tackle shop, camping equipment, and across the road on the sound side, a marina with boat ramp and boat rentals. Motels are located to the north but not within easy walking distance. The pier affords excellent flounder and red drum fishing. Because king mackerel float fishing is conducted here, various southern pelagics have been taken on live bait set-ups, including a forty-three-pound amberjack several years ago.

T5. Junco Street in South Nags Head below the Outer Banks Pier is a good general fishing location from April through November. The start and end of the season are especially good for big bluefish and other game, and the area sees little fishing pressure.

T6. Coquina beach is one of the few swimming beaches on the Outer Banks. Vehicles must park, but the walk to the surf is only about 150 feet. There is good general fishing for pompano, small bluefish, whiting, and flounder during the season, and big chopper bluefish often hit the beach in April and again in October or November.

T7. North Beach at Oregon Inlet provides excellent general fishing from April through November, and large schools of spotted sea trout or big bluefish

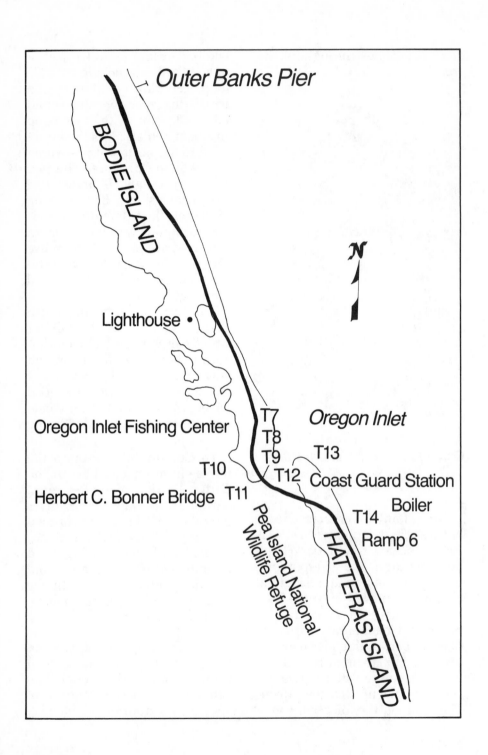

are likely to hit the beaches in spring and fall. The water is oceanic on an incoming tide, rather than muddy, and fishing on North Beach can be very different from the action on other beaches ringing the inlet. There is ready access to this beach from the federal campground at Oregon Inlet.

T8. North Point at Oregon Inlet offers good surf fishing for pompano and flounder during much of the season and is one of the premier locations for large chopper bluefish and hordes of sea trout during November and part of April. This is a popular beach for people camping at the federal campgrounds at Oregon Inlet. The water is clear and oceanic much of the time.

T9. South Beach, on the north side of Oregon Inlet, is popular with visitors to the federal campgrounds located right at Oregon Inlet, on the ocean side of the road. The beach is often suffused with water from Pamlico Sound, muddy or loaded with grasses and debris. This is a good location for flounder and other bottom fishes (spot, croaker, gray sea trout, whiting, small bluefish) during the entire season.

T10. West Point, on the north side of Oregon Inlet, is a broad, flat area frequented by beach buggy fishermen, but there is no way for a walking angler to get there. You can see this area

48¹/₂ lb. Red Drum
Caught from the Pamlico Sound by Elvin Hooper (Photo by C. R. Cannon, Dare County Tourist Bureau)

while driving over the Herbert C. Bonner Bridge and looking west toward Pamlico Sound. The water off the beach drops suddenly into Oregon Inlet's channel, and bottom fishing for flounder, gray sea trout, croaker, spot, and small bluefish is usually good from April through November.

T11. The Herbert C. Bonner Bridge over Oregon Inlet is a huge structure, with catwalks at the north and south ends. Shoaling around the pilings since the bridge was constructed has rendered the north catwalks useless, as they now hover over marshes. The south end catwalks are not nearly long

125

enough to accommodate all the people who want to use them on weekends, but the avid fisherman will find some fine action here. There are catwalks on both the ocean and sound sides of the bridge, accessible from the parking lot (ocean side) on the south end. The currents under the bridge are very strong, and on an outgoing flow (which occurs most of the time), the water may carry a great deal of grass and other debris. That can make fishing both difficult and frustrating, for no amount of lead weight will keep your bait on the bottom when your line becomes wrapped with grass from top to bottom. The shoreline is rip-rapped with stones to protect the bridge base and retard erosion of the inlet. Further out over the water, the depth increases at the channel (which has been moving steadily southward), and the bottom is sandy. The bridge stanchions themselves are, of course, concrete. As a result of the currents, depths, and varying kinds of bottom structure or lack of it, a great variety of fishes are caught from the Herbert C. Bonner Bridge (locally just called the Oregon Inlet bridge). The rocky area close to shore yields small black sea bass, young tautog, small gag grouper, pinfish, small gray sea trout, puffers, and many small bluefish. As you get out over the sandy area, the cur-

rent becomes swift, and flounders, spot, croaker, and large gray sea trout and big bluefish become frequent. Many of the largest gray trout caught on our coast are taken here, and small ones are caught from the Oregon Inlet bridge when nobody is catching anything along the entire northern coast. Many cautious or inexperienced anglers fish from that catwalk, which will keep their lines running away from, rather than under, the bridge. However, some of the best fishing is immediately under the bridge. Large sheepshead feed on the barnacles and crabs that abound on the concrete stanchions, and big sea trout hover in the swift currents. Big flounder lie in the scoured channels feeding on baitfish swept out of Pamlico Sound. The Herbert C. Bonner Bridge attracts a lot of anglers who have neither a beach buggy nor the desire to fish from a pier. But it also attracts several area guides and local fishermen, and they usually know where to go for the best area fishing.

T12. Coast Guard Channel. Located on the south side of the bridge, the Oregon Inlet Coast Guard Station is a busy facility. Vessels operated by the Coast Guard are moored in a deep hole adjacent to the public parking lot on the south shore, and a steeply descending channel to the mooring area is located just a short distance from shore. This is a famous trout hole among local fishermen, who walk out into the water far enough to cast into the hole. That hole is dangerous, and wading is safer when the water is clear (which is seldom). You can find the margin of the channel by simply casting ahead of you and feeling the drop of your weighted terminal tackle. The edge of the channel is also good for flounder, but sea trout are the big attraction. Small boats fish the far side of this channel, while foot-bound anglers work the near side. Fishing here can be productive all season long, but May and October are particularly good gray sea trout months. If in doubt about safety, just wait until several other anglers are there defining the perimeter. This is no place to take youngsters.

T13. East Side at South Point. The ocean side of the southern shore of Oregon Inlet consists of two portions. A near portion can be reached from the Coast Guard road just south of the parking lot. There is a small parking area past the station, from which anglers can walk out to fish a narrow strip of beach along the channel. An irregular path through the brush will take you out to more easterly beach segments. That path was recently closed by the Coast Guard, whose commander must think fishermen are terrorists. All seg-

ments can be productive but they often differ in the quality of water moving across the beach. In April and again in November, big chopper bluefish move in close to the beach in pursuit of baitfish, and large channel bass sometimes pass close to shore as they migrate in or out of Pamlico Sound. During the intervening months, this entire area provides good action for small bluefish, puppy drum, flounder, spot, and occasional sea trout.

T14. The Boiler, located off Ramp 6 at the north end of Hatteras Island, is a good spot for large red drum and big bluefish in April and November. During the intervening season there is good action for spot, croaker, flounder, and pompano on the bottom, while small bluefish and Spanish mackerel can be taken by casting lures past the waves.

Hatteras Island Fishing Pier, Rodanthe, N.C. 27968, telephone (919) 987-2323. It was the middle of the night on November 7, 1973 when Elvin Hooper hooked and landed a ninety-pound red drum, establishing a new world record that would last eleven years. Although landing a record fish is a rare event, catching twenty to thirty big drum in the 30- to 50-pound range is not remarkable on the Hatteras Island Fishing Pier. During a three-day run in 1984, more than 140 big red drum were decked (almost all of them

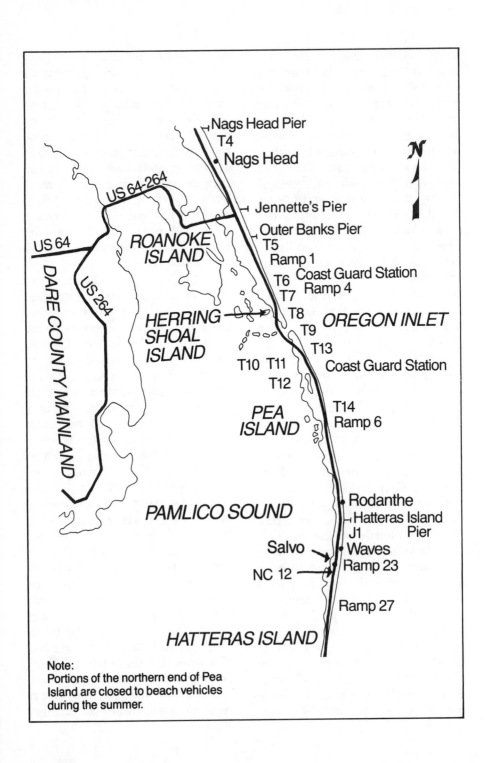

Nags Head Pier
T4
Nags Head

US 64-264

Jennette's Pier

US 64

ROANOKE
ISLAND

Outer Banks Pier
T5
Ramp 1
T6   Coast Guard Station
T7   Ramp 4

US 264

HERRING
SHOAL
ISLAND

T8
T9   OREGON INLET
T13

DARE COUNTY MAINLAND

T10 T11
T12

Coast Guard Station

PEA
ISLAND

T14
Ramp 6

PAMLICO SOUND

Rodanthe
Hatteras Island
J1   Pier

Salvo   Waves

NC 12   Ramp 23

Ramp 27

HATTERAS ISLAND

Note:
Portions of the northern end of Pea
Island are closed to beach vehicles
during the summer.

released). The 1,100-foot fishing pier was first built in 1960 and has been very well maintained. On the pier is a well-stocked bait-and-tackle shop and restaurant. The complex includes a motel, cottages, and efficiency apartments. There are additional accommodations in the town of Rodanthe.

Although the pier is most famous as a fall red drum pier, many other kinds of fish are taken here as well. The sloughs and bars off the Hatteras Island beach swarm with bluefish, flounder, spot, croaker, puppy drum, pompano, gray sea trout, and sea mullet. Spring and fall invasions of giant bluefish, often accompanied by hordes of little tunny, sweep beneath and around the pilings. The pier is sufficiently far from its neighbors to the north and south that what is happening on all of them may be quite different.

55¹/₂ lb. Channel Bass
Caught by Dominic Quattrone at Cape Hatteras (Photo by Ray Couch, Dare County Tourist Bureau)

J1. Ramp 20 just below Rodanthe provides access to a beach segment very good for big bluefish in the spring and fall. In the same area, another good location is the beach off Ramp 23 at Salvo. There are some other ramps in this area, the numbers corresponding to mile markers rather than to the quantity of ramps. Various ramps may be open or closed by the National Park Service at different periods for maintenance or because of erosion problems, but the entire area is virtually equivalent.

Ramp 34 at Avon. The holes north of the Avon Pier are often muddy and discourage fishermen from sticking around. But they also attract calico crabs in the fall, and the crabs attract foraging red drum. They also attracted David Deuel, who caught his IGFA all-tackle world record 94-2 red drum from one of these holes in 1984. Deuel used a Daiwa eleven-foot surf spinning rod and Daiwa 7000 reel filled with seventeen-pound-test Stren monofilament line. At the end of a 27¹/₂-foot shock leader, Deuel tied a fish-finder rig and baited the 8/0 hook with a mullet head.

Avon Pier, P.O. Box 160, Avon, N.C. 27915, telephone (919) 995-5049. After suffering severe storm damage in 1980-81 that restricted its use by red drum fishermen, the pier reopened under new management in 1983. The current pier is 810 feet long from the parking lot ramp, with a 90-foot T-section on the end. Facilities include a full-line bait-and-tackle shop, a seafood restaurant featuring steamed crabs and shrimp (hard to find on the Outer Banks) and all kinds of Gulf Stream specialties, a fresh seafood market for the benefit of those cooking nearby, and a campground with thirty-eight full-hook-up sites. There are additional accommodations in the town of Avon and at Buxton six miles to the south. Fish taken here during the season include abundant puppy drum, a few big red drum, spot, small bluefish, sea mullet, and croaker. King mackerel and cobia are taken in spring and summer by float fishermen working the T-end, and the big chopper blues and pods of little tunny come by in April and late November or early December.

J2. The surf on either side of the Avon Pier is excellent for big red drum. On November 12, 1983, Lyn Gottert of West Virginia broke a five-year-old IGFA women's twenty-pound-line class record for red drum with a 65-pound beauty. When the big drum are not there, myriad flounder often are so thick in the surf that they can be snagged by jerking heavy Hopkins squids with sharp treble hooks along the sandy bottom.

J3. The beach north of Ramp 38 has a nice hole that provides good flounder fishing in the fall.

J4. Get on the beach via Ramp 38 and drive south until you come to a barrier of wooden posts blocking further vehicular travel. From here you can see and walk to a very large, broad hole, excellent for big red drum and spotted sea trout (specks) in the fall. Not a typical slough, because there doesn't appear to be any major bar close in, this is one of the best deep red drum depressions anywhere on Hatteras Island. The hole is abutted by complex, almost riverlike, shoals to the north and sometimes the south, which abound in flounder on an incoming tide.

J5. Between Ramps 38 and 41 is a parking area turnout with a walkway for footsloggers. Walk out to the beach and then turn north, and you will come to another excellent hole located south of the one recommended in J4.

J6. Buxton and vicinity. Often overlooked is the beach area behind the motels in Buxton. If you're staying at one of the motels, leave your vehicle in the lot and just walk out to the shore. The entire beach is excellent for flounder and big bluefish in the fall, and pompano and other surf fish all during the summer. In December of 1983, one surprised angler landed a thirty-eight-pound black drum, a fish not normally found here. In fact, even large sharks can be taken from this beach.

In the middle of Buxton you will find the road leading to the Cape Hatteras Lighthouse. You

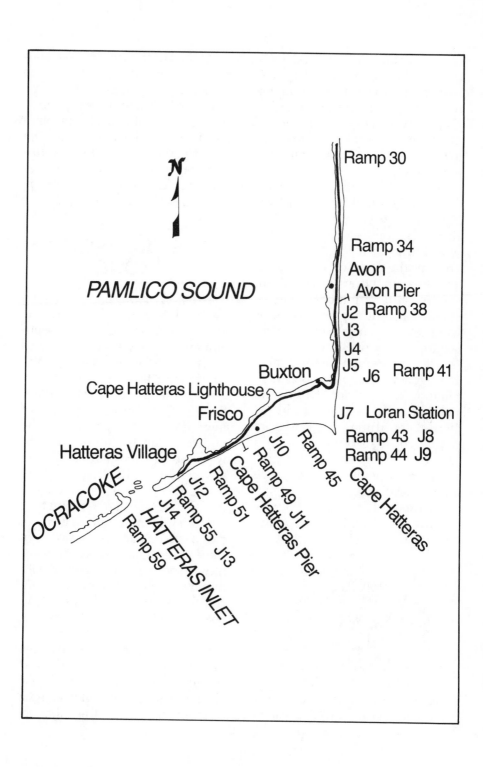

can park your car here and walk out on this very narrow beach, which excludes beach buggies (because of erosion problems). There is very good fishing south of the wooden breakwater that extends straight out from the lighthouse.

J7. South of the Cape Hatteras Lighthouse is the "Loran Station." Drive up on access Ramp 43. You don't need a four-wheel drive to reach the parking area at the foot of the dunes. There is no Loran transmitting station here anymore, only a small, flat building way back in the sandy marshlands of the island, where one or two lonely Coast Guardsmen man a new Emergency Response Network Station. You can see it from the parking area on the landward side of the dunes but not from the beach. Just to the north you will find a big slough that extends a considerable distance along the beach. This is a popular area for flounder, puppy drum, red drum, and spotted sea trout (specks).

14 lb. Weakfish

Former N.C. State Record – Caught by Pauline Hess at Hatteras Island

J8. North Beach is that segment of the shore between the Loran Station slough and Cape Point. In addition to being one of the prime locations for big blue-fish in April and November, the very steep beach produces abundant big flounder well into December. You can get here by turning south from Ramp 43.

THE TRANSITION ZONE

The transition zone between the Mid-Atlantic Bight and the South Atlantic Bight is a turbulent area of dangerous capes and violent storms. Here, the southward flowing coastal current of the northern Mid-Atlantic Bight, with its baggage of migrating sand, crashes into the South Atlantic Bight's northward flowing coastal current in an endless battle that has produced three capes and shoals as the discards of their stalemate.

From inland, an entire army of rivers crashes down the slopes of the Appalachians, draining piedmont and coastal plain of silt, minerals, and nutrients to fertilize the sounds, estuaries, and coastal wetlands of both Carolinas.

Offshore, almost directly east of Charleston, the northward rushing Gulf Stream violently sideswipes a huge undersea rock outcrop known as the Charles-

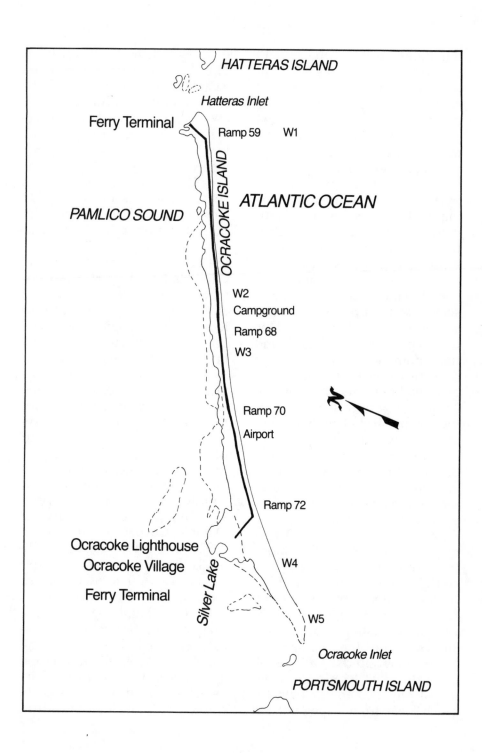

ton Bump, causing the current to swirl up sediments and nutrients from the bottom and creating an upwelling to the northeast. The twisting current gets added spin as it hits the three capes, causing more upwelling all along the North Carolina coast. The upwelling of nutrient-rich bottom water mixing with warm South Atlantic Bight water and cold Mid-Atlantic Bight water creates a milieu teeming with plankton and the creatures that depend upon it.

Fishermen pulling beach seines come up with colorful southern box crabs in the same haul with northern bluefish and think nothing of it. It has always been this way here, where two great bights meet. There are no "typical" fish of this area, just as there is no sharp line that determines where one species' distribution ends and another's begins. This is a violent feeding ground for the strongest predators, a trap for the weak, a graveyard for the unlucky.

From the land-based fisherman's point of view, the transition zone begins where the straight north-south coastline comes to an abrupt end at Cape Hatteras and turns sharply westward. Fishing is completely altered, with the winds now having new effects. Ollie Jarvis of Buxton ("J" locations on the maps) provided information for beach areas from Cape Hatteras

to the south end of the island. The hot spots for Ocracoke Island were provided by Ocracoke surf guide Wayne Teeter ("W" map locations). Surf fisherman Bernie McCants offered his lore ("M" map locations) for lonely Portsmouth Island. For the Cape Lookout area, hot spots were provided by guide Howard (Butch) Henderson ("B" map locations) of Morehead City.

The center of activity in the Cape Hatteras area is at Buxton, where a sharp bend in the road announces an expansion of Hatteras Island providing anchorage for the Cape Hatteras Lighthouse and the town's residents. A short series of motels and tackle shops famous for guide service and custom rods border the road. Everyone knows everyone else, and residents bend over backwards to show visitors the quality of life. For guide services, check with Ben Doerr at P.O. Box 329, Avon, N.C. 27915, tel. (919) 995-5345; Ollie Jarvis at Dillon's Corner, Buxton, N.C. 27920, tel. (919) 995-5083; Fishing Unlimited, Buxton, tel. (919) 995-5224; or The Red Drum, Buxton, tel. (919) 995-5414.

J9. Cape Point is probably the most heavily fished, and invariably crowded, hot spot in the Carolinas. Weekends during the spring and fall are marked by vehicles parked almost door to door, and anglers standing shoulder to shoulder fish a spider web of monofilament lines into the red sunrise. Knowledgeable anglers fish Cape Point only at the right times, avoiding the crowds as much as possible.

To fish Cape Point, watch the wind. Look for a west or southwest wind to bring in muddy water and baitfish from Hatteras Inlet. Big drum will mix with the baitfish if the wind is strong and the beach turbulent. When the wind switches and comes from the east, the muddy water washes out to be replaced by clear oceanic water, but the baitfish remain. On the heels of the water change, look for big bluefish to hit the beaches in pursuit of the bait.

J10. South Beach is the area immediately below Cape Hatteras, reached by Ramp 45. You can also drive around from the northern ramps. Popular with red drum fishermen in the spring and fall on a west or southwest wind, it is also good in the summer for spot, croaker, and pompano, and in the fall for puppy drum and flounder.

At this point, let's review the places to fish on different winds. If the wind is out of the northeast, Ollie Jarvis recommends fishing False Point (J14, below). If out of the southwest, go to Cape Point (J9) or North Beach (J8). A northwest wind is good only if it comes after a southwest wind to bring bait to the Point

from Hatteras Inlet. Finally, a wind out of the southeast will produce good fishing anywhere in the area.

J11, Ramp 49; J12, Ramp 51. These ramps are close together behind Billy Mitchell Airport, although the beach in front of one may be hotter than that in front of the other at any specific time. Check them both out. Usually overlooked by visiting fishermen, this area provides outstanding late fall fishing for big flounder.

Cape Hatteras Fishing Pier, Frisco, N.C. 27936, telephone (919) 986-2533. You would think that the "Frisco" pier is in just the right location for channel bass (red drum). With a length of 600 feet, the 1960-vintage pier is just a bit short of the deep offshore sloughs traversed by the schools of red drum that move between the shoals of Cape Hatteras and Hatteras Inlet. The pier is a favorite with the Virginia Beach Sharkers, who pick up whole tuna-head baits at the Oregon Inlet Fishing Center on the way down. Some monstrous catches have been made on this pier, but the management would prefer to encourage more family-oriented fishing activities. The pier produces excellent fall flounder fishing, and large numbers of pompano, sea mullet, spot, croaker, and puppy drum are taken here. One of the most action-packed fishing piers on the Outer Banks, it is equipped with a bait-and-tackle shop and grill and has a large parking area for campers.

J13. An enormous slough runs along the length of the beach, to which Ramp 55 provides access. For those without a beach buggy, the walk from the parking lot is not bad. The beach is protected on a northeast wind and is an excellent place to fish for puppy drum. Beach buggy drivers who work this beach are warned that, although you can drive from here to False Point at very low tide, you will be cut off by rising water.

J14. False Point is really the northeast side of Hatteras Inlet. The sand is dark colored, very coarse and difficult to traverse, but the beach drops suddenly into deep water, and the fishing can be excellent. False Point is best on a northeast wind since it is protected, and you can cast with the wind at your back. To drive out here, the safest access is from the Ranger Station.

The village of Hatteras offers additional services, including guides and custom tackle. Contact Fishin' Stuff Tackle Shop in Hatteras at (919) 986-2111; the Pelican's Roost at (919) 986-2213; or Hatteras Hobby and Tackle Shop at (919) 986-2520.

Ocracoke Island is accessible by free ferry from Hatteras Island (forty minutes crossing time, no reservations required) or from the mainland (two to three hours crossing time). If you're departing from Swan Quarter on U.S. 64, reserve a spot on the $10-per-car, twice-a-day ferry by calling (919) 926-1111. For those coming via U.S. 70 and Morehead City to the Cedar Island Ferry Terminal, the $10-per-car ferry space can be reserved by calling (919) 225-3551. To reserve your departure slot from Ocracoke Island, telephone (919) 928-3841.

The entire ocean beach of Ocracoke Island offers solitude and good fishing for sea mullet, pompano, and small bluefish during the summer, and other game during the spring and fall. The better locations are the ends of the island, where the inlets meet the sea. There are no fishing piers. For beach guide service, telephone Wayne Teeter (919-928-5491) or David Nagel (919-928-5351). For up-to-date information on which ramps are open, call the National Park Service at (919) 928-5111.

W1. If the wind is out of the northeast, a good spot is the tideline rip at the east end of the island, accessible from Ramp 59. The best puppy drum and big red drum fishing occurs after a hard rain, when the demarcation between muddy Pamlico Sound water and clean oceanic water is sharpest. Fishing is also good here for flounder and sea trout.

W2, W3. The beaches to the north and south of the campground at Ramp 68 are often

136

good for little bluefish, spot, croaker, sea mullet, and other small game. Try both locations, as beach fish tend to move in packs.

W4. Take Ramp 72 right outside Ocracoke Village at the west end of the island (called the "south" end by natives), and you will see a break in the dunes. The beach in front of this dune break has good gullies, a superb slough, and there is a nice little point here for casting. This is a good location on a southwest wind.

W5. You can get on the beach from Ramp 72 and continue all the way to Ocracoke Inlet. The tip of the island is good here, too, on a southwest wind. Look for the tideline rip of sound water meeting ocean water, and fish the edge. This is a good location for flounder, big red drum, and sea trout.

Perhaps no spot is as hot for red drum surf casting as the Vera Cruz Shoal that sits right in the middle of Ocracoke Inlet. As they say in the cartoons, you can't get there from here, and that's true of the islet, unless you know what you're doing. Few people do, and that is why the only safe way to get there is under the wing of a local guide. For a very small fee, the local guides will take you to the islet during the appropriate tide by small boat, and they will bring you back when the tides and winds indicate that it is time to evacuate. Unless you are a seafaring native of Ocracoke, it is dangerous and foolish to try to reach the island on your own. Do it safely and under the watchful eye of a guide, and you will experience a wonderful trip.

Portsmouth Island (also known as Northern Core Bank) is located immediately west-southwest of Ocracoke and is reached by ferry from Atlantic, at the end of U.S. 70 beyond Morehead City. The fare is $10 per person and, if you want to bring your own beach buggy, $50 per vehicle round trip. To reserve a free beach vehicle permit, contact Cape Lookout National Seashore, P.O. Box 690, Beaufort, N.C. 28516, tel. (919) 728-2121. For ferry reservations, contact Captain Don Morris, Atlantic, N.C. 28551, tel (919) 225-4261. There are some new motel units on the island and several old cabins that can be reserved through Don Morris.

At times, the wind blows so much water out of the shallow sound that people are stuck on Portsmouth until the wind shifts and the ferry has enough water, or someone brings in an airboat. Carry plenty of provisions and don't make any appointments for the day after your scheduled trip!

Two guides are licensed to work this national seashore and can provide everything you need, including the use of a permitted beach buggy. Contact

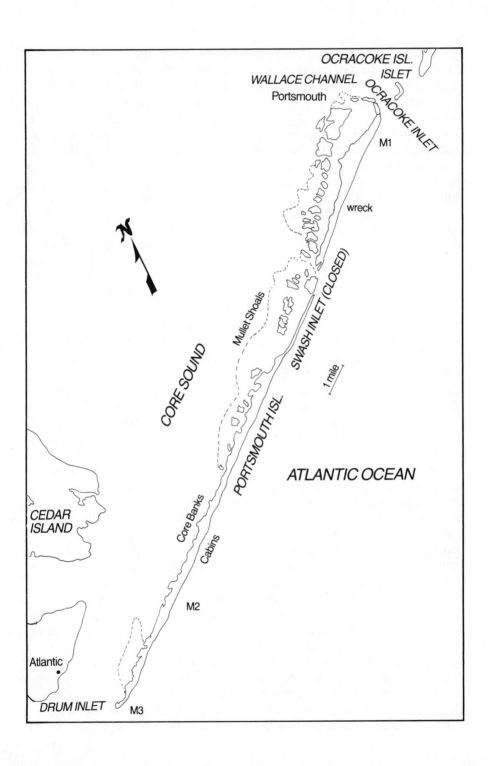

Butch Henderson, 109 North 23 Street, Morehead City, N.C., tel (919) 726-7532; or David Willis, c/o EJW Bicycle Shop, 2206 Arendell Street, Morehead City, N.C. 28557, tel. (919) 726-4725 and -9848. For further information, contact Pete Allred at Pete's Tackle Shop, 1708½ Arendell Street, Morehead City, N.C. 28557, tel. (919) 726-8644.

M1. The northeastern third of Portsmouth Island, from the tip to the submerged wreck that is visible at low tide, is a good area for large red drum from April through June, especially on a southwest wind. Good sloughs can develop anywhere along this stretch, so learn to read the beach for sloughs and rips where drum are likely to be feeding. While you are up in this part of the twenty-two-mile-long island, wander through the deserted ghost town of Portsmouth and feel the mortality of a long gone community.

M2. From the Kabin Kamps operated by Captain Don Morris, it is approximately five miles to the southwest end of the island at Drum Inlet. Along the last three miles of this beach you will find additional sloughs that offer good puppy drum fishing in the spring and again in the fall.

M3. At the far southwest end of the island is a vast expanse of shallows known as New Drum Inlet. It has always been an ex-cellent location for huge hordes of puppy drum in the spring and flounder in the fall, and catches of a few hundred pounds per person in a few days are not unusual. It was greatly deepened during Hurricane Gloria in 1985 and might not yet be back to normal. The best surf fishing is on a northeast wind when, with the wind at your back, it is very easy to make long casts. Boaters come here from Atlantic to drift fish for flounder, as New Drum Inlet is one of the top flounder locations in the state.

Just below New Drum Inlet is Southern Core Bank, the twenty-one-mile-long island root of Cape Lookout. Famous for puppy drum, flounder, occasional runs of big bluefish, and a great variety of other surf game, this part of the Cape Lookout National Seashore is managed for the benefit of wildlife, fishermen, birdwatchers, and other nonconsumptive and nondestructive users. A few years ago, the feds proposed restricting access to this island, eliminating beach vehicle traffic, and began removing old abandoned vehicles and non-native vegetation, in an attempt to return the island to its original condition and to protect sea turtle and sea bird nesting sites. The feds soon gave up on vehicle removal because the expense was eating up their entire budget. This generated a great deal of discussion among environmental groups and fishing clubs, and a sensible modification was found that pleased all users and protected the resource for native species. Recreational fishermen organized a massive volunteer clean-up effort and managed to dig out and remove all the old vehicles that remained. The abandoned vehicles and much non-native vegetation have now been removed, but nesting areas are protected, and access for vehicles is by permit only.

Much of the island offers fine surf fishing, but three locations must be considered best. First, the northern part of the island at the south end of New Drum Inlet is a good location for flounder and puppy drum, but difficult of access. At the other end of the island, the east side of the point provides good chopper bluefish action in spring and fall, while the south side is often spectacular for puppy drum, gray sea trout, and flounder. The length of the island offers fine fishing for flounder and sea mullet all season long.

Access to Southern Core Banks is from two locations. If you're a foot fishermen, you can take the $10 (adult; $5 child) round-trip ferry from Harkers Island Fishing Center (919-728-3907). It runs at least twice a day, with one trip going at 9 a.m. and returning at noon, and a second ferry going over at 1 p.m. and

returning at 4 p.m. The Harkers Island ferry lands on the eastern shore of Bardens Inlet, and from here a tractor-drawn sled carries fishermen to and from various locations along the beach. If you want to carry a beach buggy or pop-up camper-trailer to the island, you'll have to take Alger Willis' ferry from Davis (919-729-2791). Willis will put you on Single Point, about seven miles below Drum Inlet. Rates are $10 round trip per person, $50 round trip for a vehicle, and $30 round trip for a pop-up camping trailer of up to 2500 pounds. For details, write to Alger Willis at Box 234, Davis, N.C. 28524.

West of Cape Lookout is Barden Inlet, the route from Harkers Island to Cape Lookout Bight for boaters. The land west of Barden Inlet is Shackleford Banks, to which there is no access unless you're a sea turtle. About eight miles in length, Shackleford ends at Beaufort Inlet in a marshy area that is unsuitable for surf fishing, even if you could get there.

Across Beaufort Inlet is Bogue Banks, popular with tourists, fishermen, and giant game fish.

Fort Macon State Park occupies the eastern shore of Bogue Banks and absorbs an enormous influx of visitors from the unbroken chain of condominiums that have marred the last remaining segments of open beach. Popular with tourists, the park

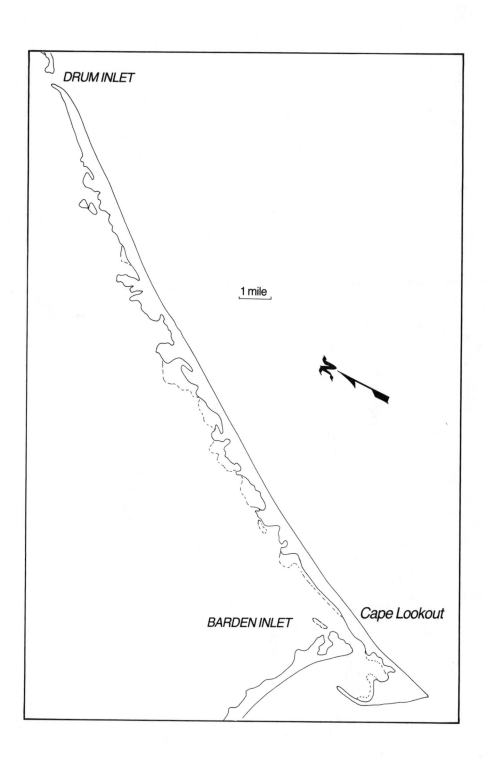

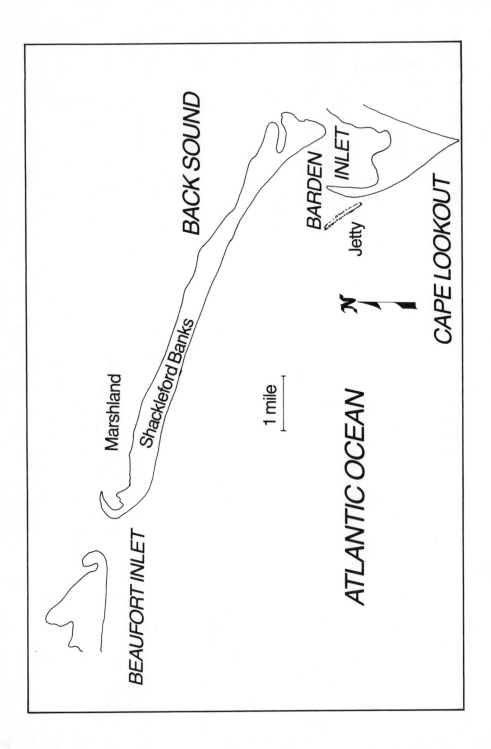

offers a protected shallow swimming beach and an extensive rock jetty from the point to the inlet. Although the jetty ought to enhance fishing, not very many notable fish are taken here. The substandard fishing may be due to heavy boat traffic, the lack of extensive rocky bottoms, or the lack of any nearby grass flats. In any case, crowds make Fort Macon State Park a poor choice for surf fishermen. On the other hand, you can shark fish from shore in the park, while sharking is no longer allowed on any of the piers because of the heavy use of the beach by swimmers.

The eight piers of Bogue Banks have seen some of the largest amberjack and tarpon to be caught anywhere in the Carolinas, and they are caught here with regularity. The piers begin after you have passed the state park. For information or fishing reports from Bogue Banks, contact Freeman's Discount Tackle on the Atlantic Beach Causeway (919-726-2607), Pete's Tackle Shop, or the EJW Bicycle Shop.

Triple S Fishing Pier, Atlantic Beach, N.C. 28512, telephone (919) 726-4170. The Triple S Pier was named for its builder, S. S. Stevenson of Henderson, North Carolina. Constructed in 1952, the pier is 1,075 feet long and is the pier closest to Beaufort Inlet. Being close to an inlet is always a point in favor of a pier, and this

one has the big fish to prove it. A previous North Carolina state record amberjack, a 105-pound monster, was taken in 1978 by Jack Long. Other big fish taken on the Triple S Pier include a 78-pound cobia, a 36-pound king mackerel, and a sheepshead just under 8 pounds. The pier is popular with flounder fishermen, as there are sections set aside where cast netting for live bait is allowed. Many other piers don't permit that activity.

Owned by Harry and Pat Rippy, the pier offers family campsites, a minimarket, and a tackle shop. There are abundant other facilities nearby.

Oceanana Fishing Pier, Atlantic Beach, N.C. 28512, telephone (919) 726-4111. Located a short distance west of the Triple S, the Oceanana Pier offers a motel (with free continental breakfast), beach showers and dressing rooms, and a full bait-and-tackle shop. Extending a length of 1,161 feet, the pier has seen some fine trophy fish. In 1983, Ida Wheeler decked a 44-pound king mackerel, still shy of the pier record of 51 pounds. A 76-pound cobia was dwarfed by a 300-pound hammerhead shark. Other good fish include a 62-pound amberjack, a 12-pound-6-ounce little tunny (an IGFA line class record at the time), and a 12-pound doormat flounder.

On Mother's Day in 1975, a huge school of king mackerel

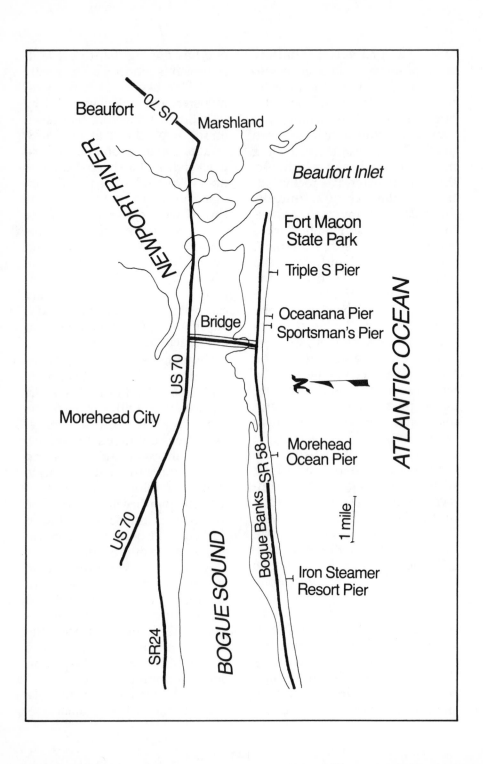

Beaufort

US 70

Marshland

NEWPORT RIVER

Beaufort Inlet

Fort Macon
State Park

⊢ Triple S Pier

Bridge

⊢ Oceanana Pier
⊢ Sportsman's Pier

ATLANTIC OCEAN

US 70

Morehead City

N

⊢ Morehead
Ocean Pier

SR 58

US 70

Bogue Banks

1 mile

BOGUE SOUND

⊢ Iron Steamer
Resort Pier

SR24

passed by this pier over a period of several hours. During the melee, anglers decked fifty-two kings and lost an uncounted number of additional fish. Nothing like this has ever been recorded at any other Carolina fishing pier.

Sportsman's Pier, Atlantic Beach, N.C. 28512, telephone (919) 726-3176. This is the third of a cluster of three piers located along a two-mile stretch near the east end of Bogue Banks. Photographs and records dating back to pier origins in 1956 were lost in a 1977 fire. The modern pier is 1,135 feet long, with depth at the end ranging from seventeen (low tide, sand bar) to twenty-seven (no sand bar, high tide) feet, according to the Army Corps of Engineers. The pier includes a restaurant and tackle shop, live bait, and overnight parking for campers.

Some of the major catches on the Sportsman's Pier include an 86-pound cobia taken in 1982 and Chris Pittman's 46-pound king mackerel taken on September 28, 1983. Several tarpon have been hooked and lost, but two at 65 and 68 pounds were caught on the same day. An amberjack just under 60 pounds was taken in 1982.

It's too bad that shark fishing is no longer allowed. On a single day back in 1967 there were eight monsters caught, ranging from 385 to 1,135 pounds.

For a stretch of almost three miles westward from the Sportsman's Pier, the beach is strictly the province of swimmers, until we arrive at that bane of surfers, the Morehead Ocean Pier.

Morehead Ocean Pier, Atlantic Beach, N.C. 28512, telephone (919) 726-5521. Owner John Robbins is well known to scuba divers and surfers for his vigorous enforcement of a clear area around the pier. He's well liked, however, by those who fish from its deck.

The pier was built in 1960 and immediately destroyed by Hurricane Donna. It was then rebuilt, all in the same year. For almost twenty years it was 1,200 feet long, with an 80-foot T at the end for king mackerel fishing. Then in the fall of 1979, it was very badly damaged by Hurricane David. At present, it is only about 800 feet long. All the piers in the Atlantic Beach area sustained considerable damage from Hurricane Gloria in 1985, but none of them was destroyed. Some fine fish taken here include a 61-pound black drum in 1965, a 94-pound tarpon in 1974, a 52½-pound king mackerel in 1973, and a 68-pound cobia in 1965.

Iron Steamer Resort and Pier, Atlantic Beach, N.C. 28512, telephone (919) 247-4213. Located about three miles west of the Morehead Pier, this fifth pier is a full resort complex that includes a motel, restaurant, bar, swimming pool, and tackle shop. The 1,000-foot-long pier has an L-extension near the surf and a small T at the end. From the 127-foot L, you can see the remains of the hull of the *Prevensey*, a British ship which supplied the Confederacy during the Civil War and which was scuttled by her crew after sustaining damage by a pursuing Union warship. The pier is dedicated as a Civil War Memorial by a marker honoring the crew of the *Prevensey*.

King mackerel float rig fishing is not permitted here. This pier allows only plugging and small game bottom fishing. A number of small kings, nice bluefish, and other game have been taken plugging. An 86-pound tarpon caught here is on display at the pier house. In 1983, two cobia of 30 and 50 pounds were taken, the former while plugging for Spanish mackerel with light tackle.

Indian Beach Fishing Pier, Route 3, Box 800, Morehead City, N.C. 28557, telephone (919) 247-3411. Almost 1,500 feet long, the Indian Beach Pier, constructed in 1974, is the sixth pier along Bogue Banks, and one of the longest and newest piers on the coast. Located some two and a half miles west of the Iron Steamer Resort and a mile east of the Emerald Isle Pier, it has one of the best tarpon records of any pier in our area. The smaller tarpon taken here include two at

74 pounds in 1977 and 1982 and a monster of 164 pounds taken by John Freeman in 1978. That fish ran out some six hundred yards of line. Several king mackerel in the 40-pound class have been taken here, but the greatest kingfishing occurred in 1983, when 160 of these game fish were landed.

Emerald Isle Fishing Pier, Emerald Isle, N.C. 28557, telephone (919) 354-3274. Located about a mile west of the new Indian Beach Pier, the Emerald Isle Pier is one of our oldest piers. Its predecessor was Thompson's Steel Pier, destroyed by Hurricane Hazel in the fifties. Today's Emerald Isle Pier is 900 feet long and has a grill and tackle shop. The Emerald Isle area is loaded with camping and motel sites and restaurants and is very popular with vacationers on various kinds of budgets. The beach is nice for swimming and is monitored by a lifeguard. Some of the larger fish taken here include a 75-pound amberjack, a 142-pound tarpon, 12- to 15-pound flounders, a 45-pound king mackerel, and a 64-pound cobia.

Bogue Inlet Pier, Emerald Isle, N.C. 28584, telephone (919) 354-2919. The eighth and final pier on this island is the 1,000-foot-long Bogue Inlet Pier. Located three miles east of the end of Bogue Banks and five miles west of its closest neighbor, this is the only pier near the inlet of

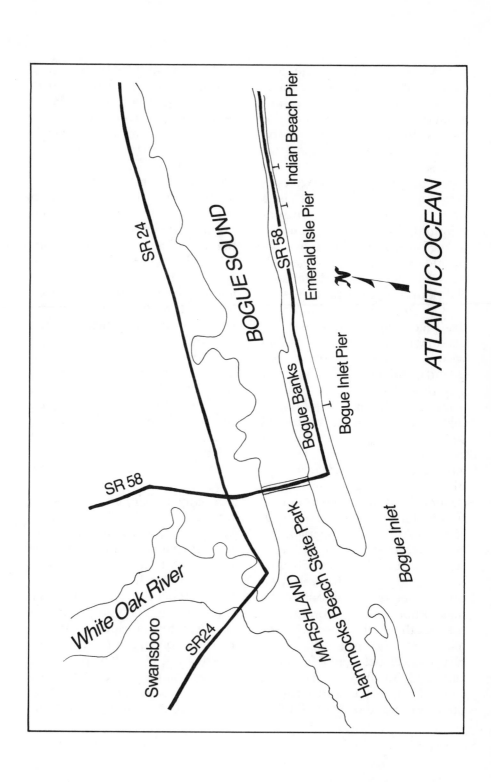

the White Oak River. The pier complex includes a tackle shop, a new restaurant, and a campground. Nearby are two major motels (the Sandra Dee and the Islander) and other camping facilities.

Several years ago, on two consecutive days, a couple took a pair of monster flounders weighing 14½ and 15 pounds. Other big fish here include a 58-pound king mackerel, a 98-pound tarpon, and Tim Stanley's 300-pound tiger shark (just a baby). Tom Jones, who fishes this pier regularly, has seen cobia down among the pilings that would easily go over 100 pounds, but nobody could ever stop those fish.

Located adjacent to the Bogue Inlet Pier is a long stretch of beach providing good flounder and sea mullet fishing. The extensive oceanfront area is popular with campers and surf casters. The major facility here is the Holiday Trav-L-Park (919-354-2250). Closer to the inlet, the beach becomes marshy and inaccessible. State Highway 58 now turns sharply northward and bridges Bogue Inlet in one of the most photogenic panoramas in the South as it crosses to the mainland and intersects with Highway 24 between Morehead City and Swansboro. Thus we come to the western end of Bogue Sound and Bogue Banks.

The nine-hundred-acre island adjacent to Bogue Banks is part of Hammocks Beach State Park, reached by free ferry off Highway 24 from June through August (Route 2, Box 295, Swansboro, N.C. 28640, tel. 919-326-4881). Flounder fishing is superb along the many deep channels just off Bear Beach fronting the ocean, and along the east (Bogue) and west (Bear) inlets. This is the last island for quite a distance, for now the mainland meets the oceanfront in a mixture of beach and marsh not open to the public. The first four miles is a military bombing area that includes land, beach, and sea from Bear Inlet to Brown's Inlet. This is a small segment of Camp LeJeune Marine Base, which extends some twelve miles to New River Inlet.

The ocean strand from New River Inlet to New Topsail Inlet is highly developed with beach houses, motels, and restaurants, yet loggerhead sea turtles somehow manage to crawl onto the beaches for nesting in the earliest morning hours before even the beachgoers and fishermen have risen. Development is heaviest to the southwest and considerably lighter toward the north. Eight ocean piers are mapped along the twenty miles of seashore, but only six of them remain open to the public. State

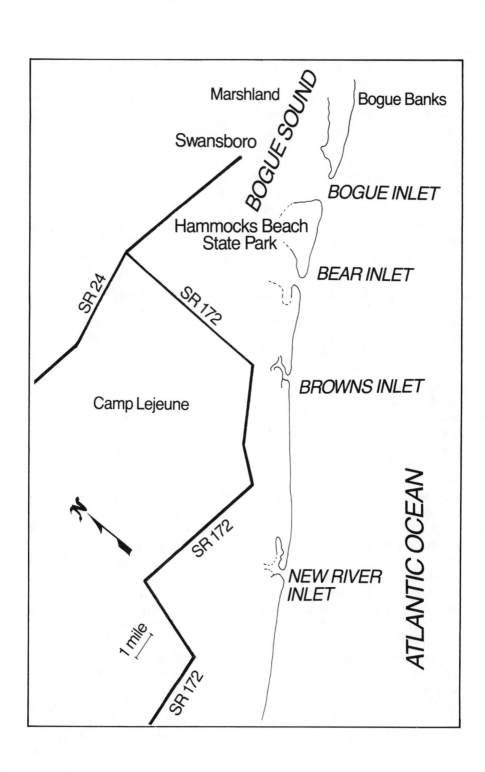

Roads 50 and 210 run the length of the beach strand, and no pier is too far away.

New River Inlet Ocean Pier, Surf City, N.C. 28445, telephone (919) 328-0154. Located at the end of the road and about a mile from New River Inlet, this is the northernmost pier in its cluster. Built in 1960, it was destroyed just two weeks later by Hurricane Donna. Rebuilt, it was known as McKee's Pier until 1983–84, when it came under new management and a major construction program was initiated. The pier is 1,450 feet long, with a wide T at the end, and features a new restaurant and motel (under construction at this writing), tackle shop, and expanded grill. Sharking is not permitted. King mackerel fishing is allowed only during daylight hours. The pier is built over a rocky bottom and produces great catches of black drum (a 43½-pounder was taken here), big flounder, scads of sheepshead, and some big cobia. An 86-pound tarpon was caught in 1983.

Paradise Pier, Surf City, N.C. 28445. No telephone at present. At this writing, the Paradise Pier had just suffered a devastating fire, and there is no word yet on when it will reopen. In 1977, a monster 159-pound tarpon was caught here, and in September of 1978 another brute weighing 124½ pounds was decked. Let's hope this pier reopens soon.

Ocean City Pier, Surf City, N.C. 28445, telephone (919) 328-5701. Dating back to 1952, the Ocean City Pier has been rebuilt several times following Hurricane Hazel and other big storms. The pier is 900 feet long with eighteen to twenty feet of water at the end. The inshore part of the pier traverses a sand bottom, but farther out the seabed becomes rocky. Featuring a tackle shop, a twenty-four-unit motel, and a restaurant, the Ocean City Pier is fully equipped for modern pier fishing. Sharking is not allowed. The largest king mackerel caught float fishing was 32 pounds. Other big fish here include a 10-pound flounder and a 73-pound amberjack. Excellent for speckled trout, large numbers of 3- to 4-pounders are caught in November on live shrimp, MiroLures, and Mr. Twisters.

Scotch Bonnet Pier, Surf City, N.C. 28445, telephone (919) 328-4261. Built in 1966 and named for the official state seashell of North Carolina, the Scotch Bonnet Pier is the newest pier in the Topsail–Surf City area. At 1,000 feet in length, it extends into twenty-five feet of water and would have been longer and deeper, but the rocky bottom at this distance would not allow the placement of additional pilings. Facilities are extensive and family-oriented, including a tackle shop, gift shop and arcade, a bathhouse with twelve

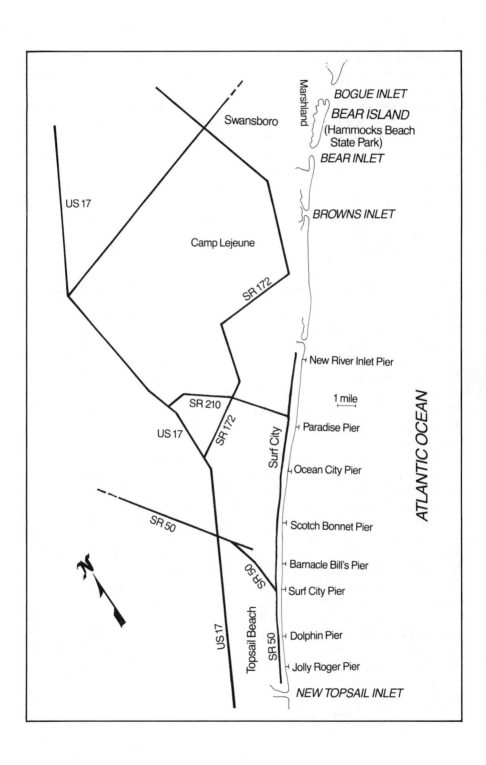

showers and sixteen lockers, a restaurant with oyster bar and 200-seat dining room, a lounge, a 62-site campground (half with full hookups) and 155-site trailer park, a lifeguard-protected beach, water slide, patio, and picnic tables. A motel is right next door.

Some large fish have been brought up on the Scotch Bonnet's decks, including 12-pound sheepshead and 12-pound flounder, a 52-pound king mackerel and a 62-pound cobia in 1977, and a 141-pound tarpon in 1980. King rig fishing is allowed at all times, including weekends. Although a 430-pound shark was caught here, shark fishing with big baits on the bottom is not permitted. Small game fishermen will appreciate the automatic fish scalers near the cleaning sinks.

Barnacle Bill's Pier, Surf City, N.C. 28445, telephone (919) 328-3661. Well known for the sheepshead and flounder fishing around its pilings, Barnacle Bill's Pier has seen a lot of other big fish come up on its decks. An 86-pound tarpon was landed in 1983 and a state record 21-pound tripletail in 1967. Other top fish include a 52-pound king mackerel and a 34-pound crevalle jack. About 300 feet from the end of the 1,000-foot pier, the sandy bottom drops suddenly to a thirty-foot rocky outcrop, popular with sport divers. The rocky

reef provides a source of sheepshead to the pier pilings, while an inshore slough provides good pompano fishing. Shark fishing is not allowed.

Built in 1958 and rebuilt in 1961, the pier today is equipped with a tackle shop, a gift shop and game room, a twenty-four-hour grill, a full restaurant, and facilities for campers and trailers.

Surf City Pier, Surf City, N.C. 28445, telephone (919) 328-3521. Built in 1951, this pier has been rebuilt several times because of storm damage and is now 1,000 feet long. A tackle shop, snack bar, and arcade offer conveniences, and accommodations are abundant in the area. There is a rocky bottom at the end varying from twenty to thirty feet, depending on bar formation and tides.

Shark fishing is not permitted. Because the pier is built in a cove and there is no T at its end, the management prefers to offer its regular customers priority for king mackerel fishing space and to encourage others to bottom fish. Some of the largest fish taken on this pier include a 94-pound tarpon, an 85-pound amberjack, a 48-pound king mackerel, a 34-pound crevalle jack, a 12-pound flounder, and an 11-pound sheepshead.

In 1976 an errant shrimp boat cut the pier in two, to the surprise of the skipper, the pier owner, and two insurance companies. Then there was the tractor driver who drove up to the pier gate and idled there until pier personnel walked out to inquire of him. Whereupon he replied that he was waiting for the drawbridge to open!

Dolphin Pier. Located in the Surf City–Topsail area, the Dolphin Pier has been taken over by a condominium development and is now closed to the public.

Jolly Roger Pier, Topsail Beach, N.C. 28443, telephone (919) 328-4616. The Jolly Roger Pier is one of the shorter piers in the area, just 771 feet long, but with a 40-foot T at the seventeen-foot-deep end for king mackerel fishing. It is the most southwesterly of the piers on the strand between New Topsail and New River inlets. The pier offers a motel, restaurant, tackle shop, and arcade. Originally built in 1954, the pier has been rebuilt several times after storm damage. Some of its larger fish include an 11½-foot shark on a king rig in 1984, a 50-pound king mackerel in 1978, a 54-pound channel bass, a 63-pound amberjack, a 36½-pound crevalle jack (at the time a state record), and a 75-pound tarpon. Shark fishing is not allowed.

A short distance southwest we arrive at New Topsail Inlet, a major channel into Topsail Sound and the Intracoastal Waterway. The borders of the inlet are marshy and not suitable for surf fishing. A long sand spit of a deserted beach follows for just over a mile, and then we come to Old Topsail Inlet, which is heavily shoaled. Another sandy beach follows before we arrive at Rich Inlet. There is yet another deserted island, and finally we arrive at Mason Inlet, where construction, roads, and development begin once again. The entire stretch from Topsail Inlet to Mason Inlet is devoid of roads or bridges. There is fine fishing for puppy drum, flounder, sea mullet, and gray trout in the spring and fall, pompano and Spanish mackerel in the summer, and speckled trout in the winter. These islands are frequented mostly by small boaters who troll along their lengths or put ashore to fish from the beach or work the channels near the inlets. This is also a haven for nesting loggerhead sea turtles and a variety of sea birds.

THE SOUTH ATLANTIC BIGHT

Although there is no sharply defined point that separates a northern fish population from a southern one, anglers in this part of the country generally agree that the fishes and shellfish characteristic of the South Atlantic Bight become the dominant marine creatures some-where between Cape Lookout and Cape Fear. There are numerous reasons for the change in faunal assemblage, and the proximity of the Gulf Stream is probably the least important. We should look, instead, to the prevailing winds and coastal currents moving westward across the Atlantic from the coast of Africa. Moving mostly along the equator, the winds push the waters of the Atlantic in a clockwise direction. The waters traverse the Sargasso Sea and move to the coast of North America where, blocked by the land mass, they begin a northward migration along the coast. Water circulating within the Gulf of Mexico in a similar direction washes out between Florida and Cuba and, passing through the Florida Straits, is swept up the coastline as a high-speed, warmwater current, the Gulf Stream. Continental winds dropping from the northern polar region also sweep downward and then, blocked by southern air masses and pushed eastward by the jet stream, turn north again as they move off the continent. The warm winds and currents then move inexorably northward until they reach the region of the Carolina capes, where they meet the southward-flowing coastal currents driven by the important Labrador Current.

Prevailing winds and currents shift during different seasons, and that prevents the formation of any sharp demarcation. Instead, what we find are several areas of conflict, where northward water from the South Atlantic Bight meets southward water from the Mid-Atlantic Bight and they clash, lose momentum, and drop their sand burdens. In each of the principal areas of collision we find a massive shoal extending the entire length of the battlefront, and right at the edge of the continent, the shoal appears as a cape.

We have major fisheries developed throughout this region, and where commercial fisheries have developed, sportsmen have followed. The major center of fishing activity in the northern part of the South Atlantic Bight is Wilmington, North Carolina. For fishing information and appropriate tackle and baits in Wilmington, check at Bobby's Bait and Tackle on Lake Park Boulevard (919-458-9255), Allen's on Dawson Street (919-762-2397), or Coastal Outdoor Sports on Market Street (919-686-0256). The fishing piers along the coast are good sources for information, tackle, and bait and can help you locate good surf fishing inlets. Unlike those in the northern zone, the guides in this area are all boaters, for this region is a center of king mackerel tournament activity.

We'll begin our coverage of the South Atlantic Bight with Masonboro Island, emphasizing that this is an arbitrary selection, and we could just as well have chosen Portsmouth Island below Ocracoke or Atlantic Beach below Morehead City.

From Mason Inlet to Masonboro Inlet is Masonboro Island, a stretch of beach strand that offers fine fishing for pompano and flounder from the surf or from its two ocean fishing piers. Masonboro Island's entire beachfront lies within Wrightsville Beach, which has an ordinance against shark fishing. Johnny Mercer's Pier is just south of Mason Inlet, and the Crystal Pier is just north of Masonboro Inlet.

Johnny Mercer's Pier, 23 E. Salisbury Street, Wrightsville Beach, N.C. 28480, telephone (919) 256-2743. Constructed in 1937 and rebuilt several times, the pier today is 1,000 feet long with a T at the end. The depth here is between twenty-eight and thirty-six feet, making this one of the deepest-water piers on the coast. The pier features a tackle shop, restaurant, bathhouse, apartments, and forty motel units with air conditioning and color television. And if you like it here, they'll even sell you real estate! Salisbury Street is easy to find, right across the road from the end of U.S. 74.

Some of the larger fish caught at Johnny Mercer's Pier include 81- and 101-pound amberjacks, a 66-pound tarpon, and a humongous 62-pound king mack-

erel. Visitors to the pier house will wonder about the weird-looking snapper mounted on the wall. That is a 47-pound cubera snapper which, at one time, was the world's record. Not only weren't cuberas supposed to get north of Florida, but they weren't supposed to get that big! It was topped in 1980 by a 60-pound 12-ounce fish from Miami Beach. The current record is over 121 pounds, set in Louisiana in 1983.

Crystal Pier, 703 S. Lumina Avenue, Wrightsville Beach, N.C. 28480, telephone (919) 256-2822. Originally constructed in 1939 as the Lumina Steel Pier, this rebuilt pier is located on the wreck of the Confederate ship, *Fanny and Genny*, the remains of which are on the pier's south side. The 1,000-foot-long fishing pier still has a steel foundation. The newly rebuilt pier house features a tackle shop, restaurant, and lounge, and the management also owns a motel. A 152-pound tarpon was caught in 1961. More recently, other trophies include a 65-pound cobia and a 52-pound king mackerel.

Right below the Crystal Pier is Masonboro Inlet, one of the few inlets on this part of the coast stabilized by jetties. Although you can reach the north jetty by foot, fishing here is virtually impossible because of a weir along the first two hundred feet. It is underwater at high tide and ex-

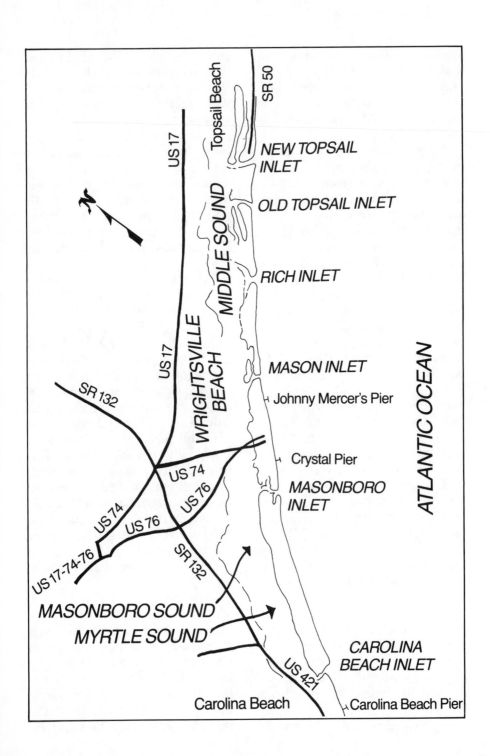

posed at other times. Across the inlet, on the south jetty, there is a walkway, and many fishermen come here to enjoy excellent trout, sheepshead, puppy drum, and flounder fishing. Unfortunately, this jetty and the adjacent beach are accessible only by boat. The remaining eight miles of beach offer good foot fishing for pompano and flounder, but again only for boaters who can put ashore here.

At the end of this island, we come to Carolina Beach Inlet, popular with surf fishermen. Although there is no access to the north side, the south side of the inlet is open to four-wheel-drive vehicles, one of the few areas on this part of the coast where beach buggies are allowed. No permit is needed.

Just the other side, development begins again as the town of Carolina Beach, and the first pier is on the ocean between Cape Fear Boulevard and Hamlet Avenue.

Carolina Beach Fishing Pier, Carolina Beach, N.C. 28428, telephone (919) 458-5518. A rocky groin abuts the beachfront at this pier, attracting lots of sheepshead, big flounder, and Spanish mackerel. There is a special fee for king mackerel fishing, and sharking is not permitted. Some large fish taken here include a 62-pound amberjack and a 51-pound cobia in 1984 and a $57\frac{1}{2}$-pound king

mackerel in 1981. The pier dates to 1947 and has been rebuilt several times following Hazel, Donna, and some bad northeasters. Originally all wood, then steel, the pier today is a mixture of materials. With a length of 1,000 feet, a bottom composed of rock, marl, and mixed materials, and a water depth of twenty-eight feet at the end, it is an important pier on this part of the coast. There is a tackle shop, arcade, and grill but no longer any campsites. The nearest motel is about a half mile distant.

Center Fishing Pier, Carolina Beach, N.C. 28428, telephone (919) 458-5739. The pier was built just before Hurricane Hazel. It is 900 feet long, extending into water about twenty feet deep at the end, where the bottom becomes rocky. Features include a tackle shop, snack bar, and seafood restaurant. Several motels are nearby. King mackerel fishing is allowed from spring to fall at all hours, but sharking is not permitted. A 90-pound tarpon was caught here, as well as a 37-pound king mackerel and cobia in the 40-pound range.

Kure Beach Pier, Kure Beach, N.C. 28449, telephone (919) 458-5524. The most southerly of three piers on this island, the Kure Beach Pier is also the oldest pier in the Carolinas, and possibly on the Atlantic coast. The original pier was constructed in 1923 of untreated wood and was 120 feet long and 12 feet wide. Fouling organisms destroyed it within a year. The following year it was rebuilt of reinforced concrete to a length of 240 feet and width of 32 feet. In all, it has been damaged and rebuilt about a dozen times. Currently it is 950 feet long over the water, rising from a high embankment. The bottom is sand and marl, with scattered rocky outcrops. The pier features a tackle shop, concession stand, arcade, and bathhouse and is associated with the Kure Key Motel. And this pier has a history. The village was developed by the Kure family, who built the pier and have retained it all these years. Currently the owners are Robertsons, and they too are part of the Kure clan.

King mackerel fishing is allowed from sunrise to sunset, May 15 through October 1. There is a live well for king mackerel baits at the end of the pier. Unlike many other piers, this one solves the problem of how many rods to allow by charging anglers a ticket for each rod they bring out on the pier. Thus, king fishermen will buy two or three tickets. Some of the better fish taken here include a 54-pound cobia and a 36½-pound king. A 29-pound crevalle jack was decked in 1983. A couple of unusual catches include a dolphin and a small sailfish that

was caught on a plug. The rocky outcrops also produce red and black drum and sheepshead. In the 1950s, as many as eighty thousand spot were landed here in a single day. In a sixty-day period in 1957, over two million fish were recorded.

Shark fishing is allowed from midnight to 6 a.m. from June 1 to September 15, but chumming is not permitted (or necessary). The state record lemon shark of 421½ pounds was caught here by Stanley Sewell in 1978, the same year that Gary Costner took a 390-pound lemon. Most sharks are 100 to 150 pounds.

The remainder of Kure Beach offers pleasant swimming and family surf fishing. Much of the beachfront toward Corncake Inlet is accessible by foot, but side roads leading toward the beach off U.S. 421 should not be trusted. Deep holes in the sandy tracks fill with rain water and remain soft for days. Rocky outcrops occur intermittently along the beach, making for fine snorkeling and good small game fishing. Pompano are abundant near the rocky areas, and good flounder can be caught close to the inlet.

The north side of Cape Fear is a marshy region known as Smith Island. It has a narrow north-south barrier beach facing the ocean. The southern or east-west side of Cape Fear is less marshy and is called Bald Head

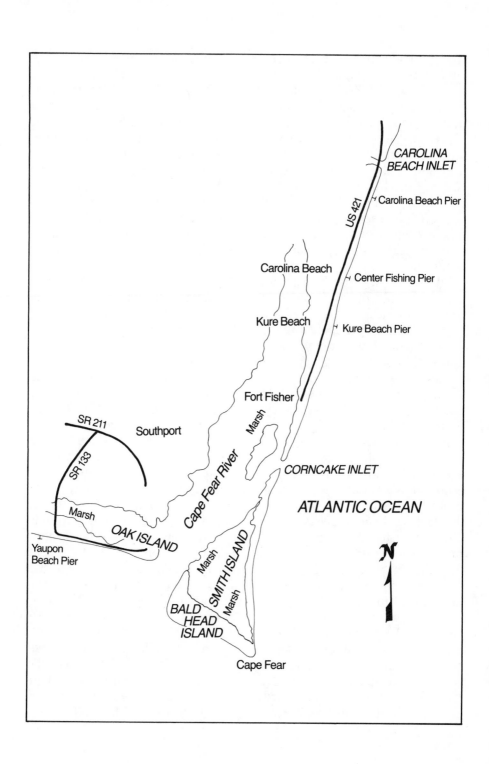

Island. The cape is really one land mass, the "islands" being defined by Bald Head Creek, the most southerly tidal creek abutting the east-west barrier island. The north side of Cape Fear is a favorite with serious fishermen. It is one of the best locations in North Carolina to fish for tarpon, but you need a boat to get well off the beach. Anglers fish a whole pinfish or hogfish on the bottom right up against the shoals.

The beach at Cape Fear is not accessible except by boat from the mainland. Some of Bald Head Island is privately owned for restricted low-density development, and other segments are managed by the Bald Head Conservancy, a part of the North Carolina Nature Conservancy. Because the island is the principal loggerhead sea turtle rookery in North Carolina, conservation agencies in and out of state government work hand in hand to protect the site. For fishermen, the lack of beach access is not important, for excellent fishing can be had right offshore or on the adjacent islands.

Across the Cape Fear River mouth on the west side of Cape Fear, the east-west shoreline begins with Fort Caswell and then continues as a series of small beach communities south and west of Southport, extending to Little River Inlet on the North Carolina–South Carolina border.

From east to west, they are Caswell Beach, Yaupon Beach, Long Beach, Holden Beach, Ocean Isle Beach, and Sunset Beach. Calabash, famed for seafood, is inland of Sunset Beach right on the state line.

The Oak Island area, at the mouth of the Cape Fear River, is strongly influenced by effluent from the river, and only gradually does the water clear as a result of the eastward flowing longshore current. Caswell Beach is often strongly subject to estuarine influence also, and it is only when we reach Yaupon Beach that the coastline is clear of the river's influence.

Yaupon Beach Pier, Yaupon Beach, N.C. 28461, telephone (919) 278-5873. The 1,100-foot pier was built in 1955, a year after Hurricane Hazel visited the area. It was rebuilt in 1972. The pier features a tackle shop, a complete seafood restaurant, an oyster roast and steam bar (manna from heaven!), a snack bar, and an arcade. Three motels are nearby. The sandy bottom becomes twenty-six feet deep at the end, and the proximity to the Cape Fear estuary provides abundant forage and big fish. Some of the top fish are a 52-pound king mackerel and a 38-pound crevalle jack. But these are dwarfed by Walter Maxwell's North Carolina state record tiger shark, caught here in 1966, of 1,150 pounds. Maxwell is no mere lucky fisherman. He also holds the IGFA all-tackle world record for a tiger shark, which he caught on another pier in South Carolina. And he says that he lost an even bigger one.

Ocean Crest Pier, Long Beach, N.C. 28461, telephone (919) 278-3798. This is the second of three piers on the island between the Cape Fear River and Lockwood Folly Inlet. It is 1,000 feet long and constructed on a sandy bottom. The pier has a motel, restaurant, and tackle shop. Shark fishing is not allowed. King mackerel fishing is exceptionally good here, where there is minimal washover of turbid water from the inlets to the east and west. The largest king mackerel taken here was a 38-pounder. In 1983, there were five hundred kings decked, including a phenomenal forty-six in a single day. In the same year, one fisherman landed a 101-pound tarpon. When the weather gets cold, look for speckled trout to 3 or 4 pounds.

Long Beach Pier, Long Beach, N.C. 28461, telephone (919) 278-5962. This westernmost pier on the island was first built in 1956 and today is 1,047 feet long. There are two motels, including a new one on the oceanfront, a restaurant, grocery, tackle shop, and campground. The big draw is king mackerel fishing, with 250 to 300 caught per year. Any angler breaking the pier record

for kings wins a lifetime pass. The top kings were two 48-pounders caught on the same day. Shark fishing is not permitted.

From the Long Beach Pier westward, the ocean beach offers good small game fishing for pompano, flounder, spot, Spanish mackerel, small bluefish, puppy drum in the spring and fall, speckled trout in the winter, and a variety of other game. The ocean front road (SR 1100) extends all the way around the tip of the island, enabling you to fish from the beach at the inlet.

The east shore of Lockwood Folly Inlet is one of the better surf fishing areas on the lower North Carolina coast. Spring and fall can be hot for flounder, blues, and puppy drum on the ocean side, but fishing becomes impossible inland, where marsh creeps out into the water. The development of marshes also makes the west side of Lockwood Folly Inlet, at the town of Holden Beach, unsuitable for surf fishing. However, the beachfront on the island is clean and sandy, and surf fishing along the open beach away from the inlet can be productive. Spring brings spot and flounder at the waveline, and pompano cruise the beach sloughs all summer and into the fall.

Holden Beach Pier, Holden Beach, N.C. 28462, telephone (919) 842-6483. Located just to

the west of Lockwood Folly Inlet, this is the only fishing pier
on sixteen-mile-long Holden
Beach Island. The 1,000-foot pier
was built in 1960 on a sandy
bottom. Conveniences include a
tackle shop, a restaurant, camping facilities, a swimming beach,
a motel, one oceanfront two-
bedroom efficiency apartment,
and a sound-side six-bedroom
cottage. A 37-pound king mackerel and a 62½-pound cobia are
notable pier records. But they
don't compare with what one
king mackerel fisherman accomplished recently. People on the
pier were watching a rare and
beautiful oceanic manta ray that
had appeared near the surface.
Circling in close to the end of the
pier, the young ray became en-
tangled in the wire and treble
hooks of a king mackerel rig.
Although an enormously powerful fish, the ray was finally sub-
dued by the angler and tipped
the scales at 237 pounds.

The rest of Holden Beach offers good surf fishing for small
game, with the action picking up
toward Shallotte Inlet to the
west. The inlet is wide and offers good action for bluefish and
pompano in the summer, flounder and puppy drum in the fall,
and speckled trout in the winter.

On the west side of Shallotte
Inlet, the broad expanse of the
virtually empty beach invites
foot-bound surf fishermen all
year. The town doesn't allow
motorized vehicles of any type

on the beach. Shallotte Point is a
favorite of surf-fishermen. The
remains of an unidentifiable
structure protrude starkly from
the sand and mark the point
where Shallotte Inlet meets the
sea. Because the inlet is about
half a mile beyond the end of the
oceanfront road, swimmers
don't swim here, and the only
nonfishermen are people walking the beach looking for shells.
The beachfront is taken up by
summer cottages and a single
pier. Shops are all located inland
along SR 904 and SR 179, and
there are few motels in the area.

Ocean Isle Pier, Ocean Isle,
N.C. 28549, telephone (919) 579-
6873. Located right at the end of
SR 904, the Ocean Isle Pier
couldn't be any easier to find.
However, fishermen looking
forward to the company of other
fishermen will be somewhat put
off by the mass of teeny boppers
jamming the arcade and grill
that must be traversed on the
way to the pier. Built in 1958, the
pier is about 1,000 feet long, has
a tackle shop, and is located on
an excellent swimming beach.
There is just one motel in the
vicinity. The paucity of accommodations limits use of this pier.
The management was unable to
provide any specifics on landings of notable fishes.

Sunset Beach Pier, Sunset
Beach, N.C. 28549, telephone
(919) 579-6630. This 1,050-footer

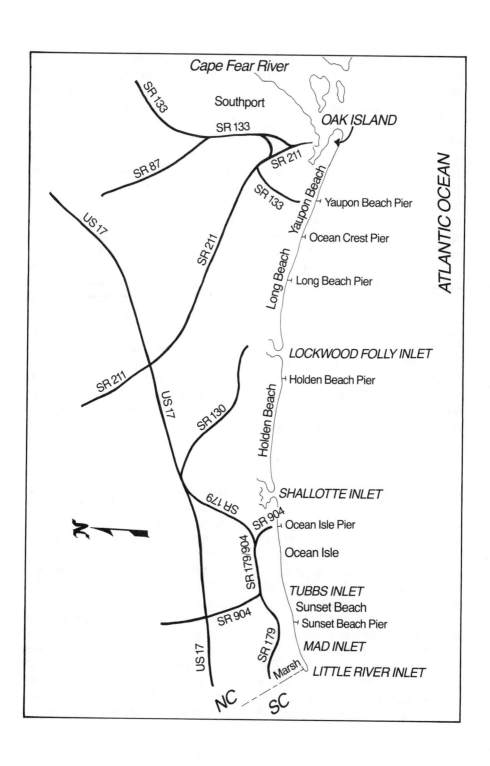

is not the original pier but a replacement a little up the beach, developed after Hurricane Hazel. The pier sits alone on the beach between Tubbs Inlet and Mad Inlet. It is also the last pier in North Carolina. There is a tackle shop, restaurant, and arcade, and two motels are located across the street. In 1983, Jerry Hunt landed a whopping 110-pound amberjack. And in the same year, a king mackerel just under 37 pounds was brought on deck.

As the frequency of inlets begins to increase, so does the occurrence of low marshes. Access roads are scarce, and the beach now becomes unsuitable for surf fishing. A short distance beyond the Sunset Beach Pier we traverse Little River Inlet and cross the state line into South Carolina.

South Carolina has more than half a million acres of coastal marshes, of which two-thirds are salt marsh. The low salt marsh is frequently inundated and characterized by smooth cordgrass, *Spartina alterniflora*, the most important sea grass on the Atlantic coast. Inland, the vegetation changes to high marsh, characterized by needlerush (*Juncus*), marsh-hay cordgrass (*Spartina patens*), saltwort (*Batis*), salt grass (*Distichlis*), glasswort (*Salicornia*), and switchgrass (*Panicum*). The cordgrasses of the brackish marshes provide most of the productivity of the state's coastal region. Seventeen distinct marshes are mapped on the South Carolina coastline, but only a few are regions where fishermen congregate. The first marsh is the one associated with Little River Inlet.

Little River Inlet Jetty offers good rock fishing, but the beach itself is not fished. The tidal river drains a moderately large estuarine area inland and toward the coast is lined on both sides by dense vegetation. Upriver just east of U.S. 17 is the port of Little River, South Carolina. Little River is the home of a fleet of commercial and recreational fishing boats, including charter craft and half-day and full-day head boats. The only general marina is Captain Small's (803-249-1222). However, the recreational fleet can also provide local information. Check in with the Little River Fleet (803-249-3970, -1824, -2845), or the headboat *Hurricane* (803-249-3571).

From Little River to Murrells Inlet, the beach is stable and the barrier island well developed with beach cottages, motels, condominiums, amusement parks, and restaurants, generally concentrated around Myrtle Beach. At one time, fishing piers were abundant in this area, but most of them have now become part of private condominium complexes and are no longer open to the public. Only two piers remain in the northern section. We begin in the north of this metropolitan area at East Cherry Grove Beach.

There used to be a public fishing pier (the Inlet Pier) just to the north of the Cherry Grove Pier (see below), but it has now become part of a condominium complex.

Cherry Grove Pier, 34th Avenue North, East Cherry Grove Beach, S.C. 29582, telephone (803) 249-1625. Built around 1952, the pier is 1,034 feet in length and has twenty feet of water at the end. The bottom is sandy throughout. Facilities include a tackle shop, a restaurant, and the Holiday House Motel. The top king mackerel at this pier weighed 42 pounds. A near record 29-pound bluefish was caught here in 1977. All these fish are dwarfed by Walter Maxwell's IGFA all-tackle world record tiger shark, a 1,780-pound monster caught on June 14, 1964. Maxwell lost an even larger one the day before. The entire exciting story appeared in the April 1984 issue of *Outdoor Life*. Maxwell also holds the North Carolina record for a tiger of over a thousand pounds taken from a pier not far to the north. Today, sharking is not allowed from any pier in the Greater Myrtle Beach area. The pier managers claim that this is based on a city ordinance, but scientists at the South Carolina Marine Resources Department were unable to find any such law on the books. According to *Outdoor Life* Senior Editor George Haas, there is fear of a hooked shark streaking past and snagging a swimmer with a trailing hook or catching him in the line or wire.

Near Second Avenue North you will see another private pier. This used to be the public Tilghman Beach Pier, but it too is now part of a condominium complex.

Holiday Inn Pier (formerly the Crescent Beach Pier), 2713 Ocean Boulevard, North Myrtle Beach, S.C. 29582, telephone (803) 272-6632. The original construction permit for this pier was issued in 1946. At one time the pier was 1,200 feet long, but it has been rebuilt numerous times after severe storms. Today it is 720 feet long. The pier is equipped with a tackle shop and snack bar and is associated with the Holiday Inn Hotel, which includes accommodations, a restaurant, and a pool. You need not be a hotel guest to use the pier. The big draw for most tourists is the abundant, tasty spot. The pier record spot is one pound, four ounces, which is two ounces larger than the official state record. King mackerel fishing is popular here, with the largest in recent years a 33½-pounder taken in 1981. A 69-

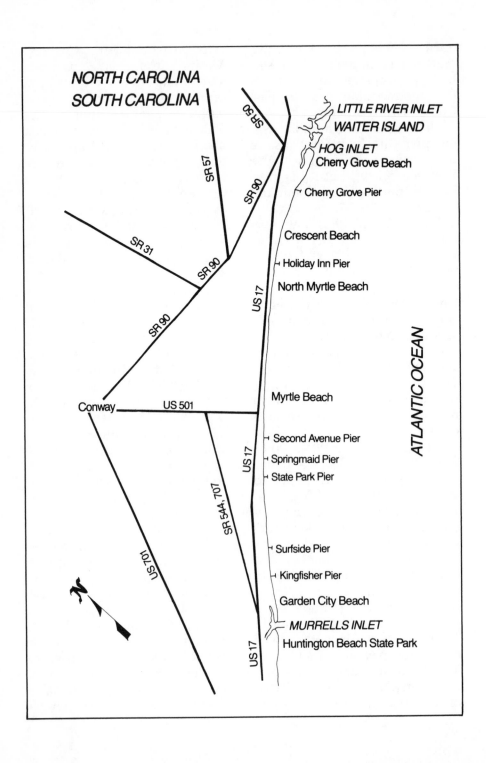

pound tarpon was decked the following year. Sheepshead and black drum in excess of 9 pounds are in the pier's record book.

The **Windy Hill Pier** at 37th Avenue South and **Kit's Pier** at 48th Avenue South in the North Myrtle Beach metropolitan area have both become associated with condominiums and are closed to the public.

We now come to a vast expanse of beach devoid of fishing piers, extending well into the next town, which is Myrtle Beach itself. Just south of the intersection of U.S. 17 with U.S. 501 from Conway, we come to the Second Avenue Pier.

Second Avenue Pier, 210 N. Ocean Boulevard, Myrtle Beach, S.C. 29577, telephone (803) 448-4241. First built in 1937 and rebuilt many times since, the pier today is only 450 feet long. Facilities include a tackle shop stocking live bait, a seafood restaurant, a lounge, a forty-eight-unit motel, and an arcade. The length makes it too short for king mackerel fishing. However, because it is built on a rocky bottom, it provides outstanding fishing for structure-loving fish. A flounder over 10 pounds was caught in 1983, and other recent catches include an 18-pound sheepshead and a 30-pound black drum. Speckled trout are caught here in the winter. Sharking is not allowed.

In 1983, unattended nets were everywhere on the beaches, and pier fishing suffered. The city of Myrtle Beach then passed an ordinance, and today nets must be no closer than fifteen hundred feet from any pier and must be attended at all times. Fishing improved dramatically in 1984.

Springmaid Pier, South Ocean Beach Boulevard, Myrtle Beach, S.C. 29577, telephone (803) 238-5212. The Springmaid Pier was built in 1972 on a sand bottom, extending 1,040 feet out to a rocky outcrop, where the water averages sixteen feet in depth. Facilities include a tackle shop, snack bar, campground, and three-hundred-unit motel. Shark fishing is not permitted. King mackerel fishing is popular here because thirty spaces are reserved, thus avoiding crowding. The top king mackerel taken at the pier was a 49-pounder. Other good fish include a 10½-pound state record Spanish mackerel and a 70-pound tarpon. Bottom fishing is also good, with flounders up to 8 pounds taken. Gray sea trout are caught in the fall and many speckled trout in the winter.

Myrtle Beach State Park Fishing Pier, Myrtle Beach, S.C. 29577, telephone (803) 238-5326. This public fishing pier is well managed by the state. It is 750 feet long over a sand bottom. Facilities include a tackle shop, snack bar, and campground with five cabins and three hundred spaces. King mackerel and small game bottom fishing are all popular here.

Surfside Pier, Surfside Beach, S.C. 29577, telephone (803) 238-0121. Built in 1952, the 850-foot-long pier covers a sand bottom, but there are rocks on the north side. Equipped with a tackle shop and restaurant, the pier is located close to numerous motels. There is no camping in this town. Sharking is not allowed. Small game bottom fishing is best in spring and fall, when big whiting and gray (summer) sea trout run. There are a few speckled trout taken in winter, but these are more likely to be found near inlets. King mackerel fishing is popular. Some of the best fish caught on the Surfside Pier include a 59-pound cobia in 1984, a 128-pound tarpon, and a 41-pound king mackerel.

Kingfisher Pier, Garden City, S.C. 29576, telephone (803) 651-9700. Most recently rebuilt in 1978, the Kingfisher is just 640 feet long and strictly a bottom fishing pier. Neither sharking nor king mackerel fishing is permitted. Large spot, whiting, and croaker are caught here (so are small ones!). A 47-pound cobia and an 8½-pound sheepshead were both taken here. The pier is associated with a time-sharing condominium complex, but rentals are available. For accommodations, telephone (803) 651-2131.

Visitors to South Carolina may marvel at Myrtle Beach, but saltwater anglers migrate to Murrells Inlet, the most intensively fished saltwater area in the state. And for good reason. This 3,330-acre community of restaurants and marinas, bounded by U.S. 17 and its business bypass, is located just a ten-minute drive from the popular resort area to the north, and tourists who come to Murrells Inlet for the famous oyster roast restaurants quickly discover its fabulous fishing opportunities. From surf and jetty fishing, to small boat, head boat, and charter boat fishing, Murrells Inlet offers it all.

The new jetties at Murrells Inlet are a bonanza for fishermen. You can reach the south jetty by walking a mile northward along the beach from Huntington Beach State Park. The north jetty is not available to foot fishermen, but the south jetty was capped in May of 1980, two and a half years after construction began. The asphalt cap extends all the way to the end, offering Murrells Inlet anglers some excellent rocky shore fishing. Best bets are spottail bass (channel bass, puppy drum, red drum) and flounders on live finger mullet taken from these waters with a cast net. For those not skilled in the art of cast netting, the shore offers killies for anyone who can drag a seine.

Sand fleas from the suds line and fiddler crabs from grassy shores are excellent baits for soft-biting, hard-fighting sheepshead, ubiquitous on the outer segment of these rocks. For anglers fishing with other natural baits, pinfish, small bluefish, black drum, and black sea bass can be taken.

If you are uncomfortable with jetties or just prefer a nice sandy beach, continue past the inlet to the next state park. Huntington Beach State Park, at the southern border of Murrells Inlet, provides shore fishermen with opportunities for whiting (sea mullet), flounder, puppy drum, and pompano that course through the wavelines feeding on sand fleas, tiny crabs, and coquinas.

For more information on fishing opportunities in the Murrells Inlet area, contact Cedar Hill Landing (803-651-5805), Captain Dick's Marina (803-651-3676), or Murrells Inlet Marina (803-651-4551 and -4451).

Thirteen miles south of Murrells Inlet on U.S. 17, we arrive at Pawley's Island. There are no fishing piers here, but good surf fishing is found all along the island, with the best locations at the north and south ends. Small red drum are sought in spring and fall, and this is a hot spot for speckled trout in the winter. For bait and tackle and information on boat rentals, contact Pawley's Island Supplies at (803) 237-2912.

Another thirteen miles to the south brings us into the Georgetown area. Charts will indicate jetties at the opening of Winyah Bay, but these are submerged and not accessible to foot fishermen. Boaters locate the jetties by the rock piles every half mile and fish at the end of the south jetty. There is surf fishing available in this area, but you need a boat to get to the beaches. The best locations are North Island, between Winyah Bay and North Inlet, and the beach segment south of Winyah Bay between the North and South Santee River mouths. The bridge over old route 17 is popular with local fishermen, but only fresh and brackish water fish occur here. For updated local information, contact the Belle Isle Marina (803-546-8491) or Georgetown Landing (803-546-1776).

Heading south once more, we pass the region of Cape Romain and Bulls Bay, where there are no facilities for shore fishing, and continue on toward Charleston Harbor.

In the Charleston Harbor area are several islands, each of them with some good fishing. On the north side of the inlet are the Isle of Palms and Sullivan's Island, accessible by taking SR 703 all the way by automobile. Between them and on SR 703 is Breach Inlet, which has a bridge with a fishing catwalk. This catwalk is popular for shark fishing, and the inlet also produces some big red drum of the size seen on the Outer Banks. There used to be a public fishing pier on the Isle of Palms, but it is now associated with a condominium complex. Nonetheless, the entire beach is good here. On Sullivan's Island, fish the far west end at Fort Moultrie for best action.

James Island is a large, well-developed coastal area abutting Charleston Harbor and is a center of fishing activity. Two bridges leave James Island and traverse Folly Creek leading to Folly Beach. The main one is part of SR 171.

Crosby's Pier, James Island, S.C. 29439, telephone (803) 795-4049. Crosby's Pier is an 80-foot-long fishing pier with a 20-foot T at the end and numerous fingers for dockage or fishing for a total of three hundred feet of dock space. It is adjacent to the other bridge and on the seaward side, rather than the James Island side. Extending into 450-foot-wide, 22-foot-deep Folly Creek, it offers anglers opportunities for spot, croaker, small sharks, and flounder. There are probably large sharks here, but nobody fishes for them. The pier offers bait, tackle, and equipment rentals, plus other services.

Folly Beach itself is well developed with streets throughout the island and ready access to the ocean surf zone. A new 2,001-foot fishing pier, park, and coastal science museum are planned for Folly Beach just south of SC 171. At the east end of Folly Beach you come to Morris Island. The rocks in front of the Coast Guard Station are a hot spot for sharks, large channel bass, bluefish, big croaker, and, although small, lots of pompano. There is deep water here. For more information on where to go and what's running, check with the Folly Road Tackle Shop (803-795-8737) on James Island and the Creekside Marina on Isle of Palms (803-886-8964).

The next area not closed to the public consists of the islands around St. Helena Sound. Between the North Edisto and Edisto rivers, the beachfront provides a few good locations for surf fishermen. Two small inlets, Frampton Inlet to the northeast and Jeremy Inlet to the southwest, are shallow, with fast-moving water, and surf fishermen here take flounders and trout in abundance. Jeremy Inlet can be waded at low tide. Southwest of the inlets is Edisto Beach. The Collins Fishing Pier here was destroyed in 1979 by Hurricane David. The southwest end of Edisto Beach is known as Big Bay Break, but locals refer to it as "Bay Point." This is a hot spot for shark fishing from the beach. The water is deep and murky, perfect for sharking from shore. The Edisto beachfront is clean and straight. Although the beach is heavily used by swim-

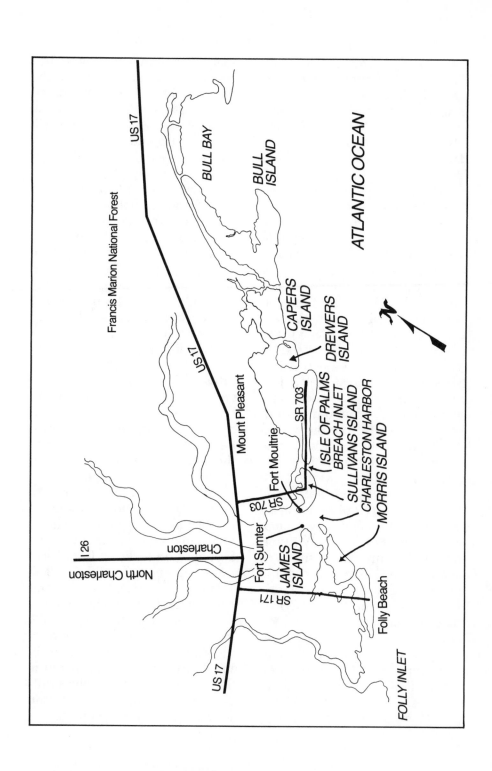

mers in the summer, it is wide open during the early spring and late fall when fishing is best. For local fishing information, check with the Stono Marina on Johns Island (803-559-2307). Accommodations are available at Fairfield Ocean Ridge (1-800-922-3330 within South Carolina; 1-800-845-8500 out of state).

Across St. Helena Sound there is a series of small islands reached via U.S. 21. The first is Harbor Island, followed by Hunting Island, which has a state park. The oceanfront on Hunting Island is very shallow and a virtual fishing desert. On the back side of the island, a channel separates Hunting Island from Harbor Island. Here anglers take spot, croaker, and spottail bass (small red drum). The best fishing on the island should be from Joe Mix's new Hunting Island Fishing Pier.

Hunting Island State Park Pier, Hunting Island State Park, S.C. 29920. Telephone Island Outfitters, the pier developers, at (803) 524-1661. At this writing, the pier is under construction and destined to be one of the longest piers on the Atlantic coast. Owner Joe Mix describes the projected pier as 1,120 feet in length, 16 feet wide over the water, extending into Fripp Inlet some three hundred yards east of the SR 406 Bridge, into about twenty-six feet of water at the end. There will be a tackle shop,

snack bar, lights for night fishing, cleaning tables, and all the usual facilities found on coastal fishing piers. Parking will accommodate 120 cars. There will be a pick-up and discharge dock for charter boats currently scattered throughout the area. The pier will take advantage of a huge resident flounder population in Fripp Inlet, currently exploited only by boat fishermen. Other fish caught here include whiting, spot, croaker, and shark. Sharking in Fripp Inlet is exceptionally good, and the pier will encourage shark fishing by hosting tournaments.

SR 406 Bridge over Fripp Inlet. Although there is no catwalk, lots of people fish here anyway, catching sharks up to two hundred pounds and sheepshead around the pilings. Be careful of traffic. Fishing on the bridge will probably halt when the pier is completed.

Across the bridge we come to Fripp Island. Although there are no facilities for beach fishing, many people do it anyway. The best location on Fripp Island is at the south end at Skull Inlet. Best bets here are trout, flounder, and small red drum (spottail bass).

You can also cross Skull Inlet to Pritchard's Island for more of the same. You cannot drive on Pritchard's Island. Just inland is St. Helena; its road parallels Pritchard's Island all the way to the shores of Port Royal Sound.

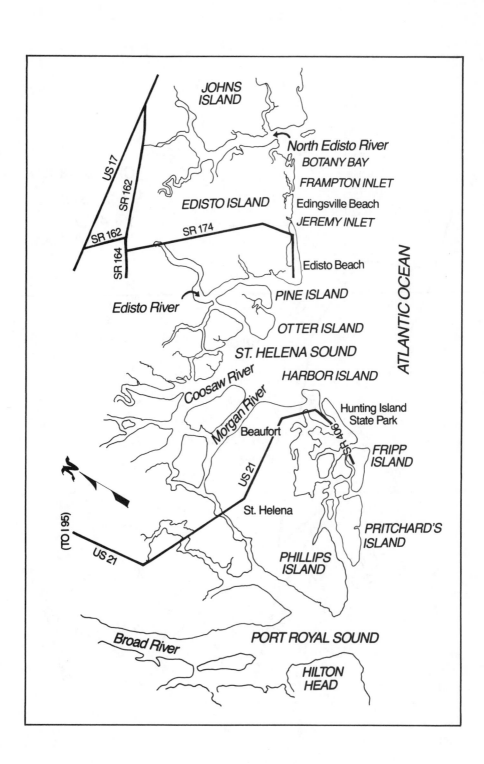

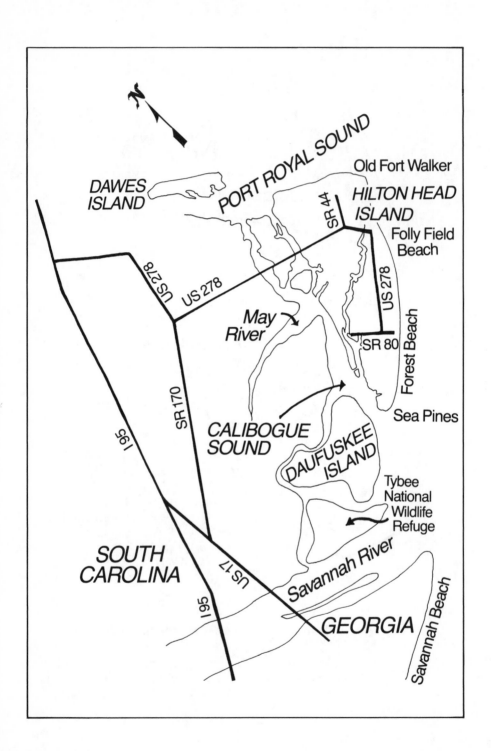

On the far side of Port Royal Sound is Hilton Head Island, an important center of offshore sportfishing activity. Hilton Head Island is on U.S. 278 east of both Interstate 95 and U.S. 17. The island has a very shallow beachfront, lacking sloughs, and is not good for shore fishing. Only two locations receive any fishing attention from the locals. The deeper location is at the south end of the island, where it meets Calibogue Sound. Another location is known as "The Folly," a spit of land extending toward the Broad River inside Port Royal Sound. Both locations offer trout, whiting, croaker, and small sharks. Note that the town of Hilton Head prohibits shark fishing from the beach or within four hundred yards of the beach. For sharking, you'll need to go to Fripp Inlet and fish the bridge or the new pier.

Beyond Calibogue Sound, we come to the end of our travels as we approach the Georgia state line.

You now have a detailed description of all the better locations on the coast of North and South Carolina and will probably never get to fish them all. However, one needs to have goals in life, and that's about as good a goal as any!

I hope you will write to me c/o John F. Blair, Publisher, 1406 Plaza Drive, Winston-Salem, N.C. 27103, informing me of major catches (with photographs), new places to fish, or the disappearance of fishing locations described in this book. Each year, some public fishing piers go private, and others are destroyed by fire or storms, or change ownership and telephone numbers. New bridges are constructed with catwalks, and new parks and jetties become available. With your help, I'd like to keep this book updated through future editions.

It's important to all of us that we have continued access to the beaches. The way to assure that is to behave in a manner that upholds respect for fishermen. That means leaving the beach as clean or cleaner than you found it, taking your litter home or back to the car. It means not killing anything you don't intend to use. It means releasing alive anything you don't want, and doing it gently. It means staying out of the way of endangered sea turtles and sea birds. It means driving only on designated ramps and roads, and staying off dunes. It means attending public meetings dealing with coastal resources, and it means getting involved with clubs and other social groups that have interests in the beaches. The beach is not ours alone but is of equal importance to other groups of people. In-

175

stead of griping about what's happening to our coast, become involved in the public business, where the various legitimate users must find a way to share the resource.

And if you're feeling down about anything, or life seems to be getting more difficult, then take this advice most of all: Take yourself fishing!

APPENDIX

MANUFACTURERS AND VENDORS OF TACKLE

Abu-Garcia, 21 Law Drive, Fairfield, N.J. 07006

Acme Tackle Company, 69 Bucklin Street, Providence, R.I. 02907

AFTCO guides. See Axelson Co.

Ambassadeur. See Abu-Garcia

Ande Lines, P.O. Box 8366, West Palm Beach, Fla. 33407

Axelson Tackle Manufacturing Co., Irvine, Calif. 92714

Bagley Bait Co., P.O. Box 110, Winter Haven, Fla. 33880

Berkley, Trilene Drive, Highway 9 and 71, Spirit Lake, Ia. 51360

Betts Tackle Ltd., P.O. Box 57, Fuquay-Varina, N.C. 27526

Comstock's Shark Tackle, P.O. Box 618, East Detroit, Mich. 48021

Conner Lures, P.O. Box 71, Buxton, N.C. 27920

Daiwa, 14011 S. Normandie Avenue, Gardena, Calif. 90249

DuPont Stren, 1007 Market Street, Wilmington, Del.19898

Fenwick, 14799 Chestnut Street, Westminster, Calif. 92683

Garcia. See Abu-Garcia

Gotcha Lures, Wilmington, N.C. 28401

Haw River Plastics, P.O. Box 2057, Burlington, N.C. 27216

Hildebrandt Corporation, P.O. Box 50, Logansport, Ind. 46947

Hopkins Lures, 1130 Boissevain Avenue, Norfolk, Va. 23507

Hurricane Rods, 5800 Miami Lakes Drive E., Miami Lakes, Fla. 33014

Jerk Jigger. See Hildebrandt

Jeros Tackle Co., Cartaret, N.J. 07008

L&S Bait Company, 1500 East Bay Drive, Largo, Fla. 33541

Lamiglas, P.O. Box U, Woodland, Wash. 96874

Lew Childre, 110 E. Azalea Avenue, Foley, Ala. 36535

Magnuflex, 3923 NW 24 Street, Miami, Fla. 33142

Mann's Bait Company, P.O. Box 604, Eufaula, Ala. 36027.

MiroLure. See L&S

Mister Twister Bait Co., P.O. Drawer 996, Minden, La. 71055

Maxima, 18239 S. Figueroa Street, Gardena, Calif. 90248

Mustad & Son, 247-253 Grant Avenue, Auburn, N.Y. 13021

Penn Reels, 3028 West Hunting Park, Philadelphia, Pa. 19132

Quick, 620 Terminal Way, Costa Mesa, Calif. 92627

Sampo, North Street, Barneveld, N.Y. 13304

Sevenstrand Tackle, 5401 McFadden Avenue, Huntington Beach, Calif. 92649

Shakespeare, P.O. Drawer S,
   Columbia, S.C. 29260
Shimano, 205 Jefferson Road,
   Parsippany, N.J. 07054
St. Croix, P.O. Box 279, Park
   Falls, Wis. 54552
Sting Silver. See Haw River
   Plastics

Walt's Walkers, P.O. Box 32,
   Manahawkin, N.J. 07762
Woodstream Corp., Lititz, Pa.
   17543
Wright & McGill Tackle Co.,
   Denver, Colo. 80216

FISHING CLUBS

(Note: For an annually updated list, contact Ron Schmied,
Special Assistant for Recreational
Fisheries, NOAA-NMFS, Southeast Regional Office, 9450 Koger
Boulevard, St. Petersburg, Fla.
33702, telephone 813-893-3141.)

Raleigh Salt Water Sportfishing
   Club
4818 North Hills Drive
Raleigh, N.C. 27612

Brunswick County Fishing Club
Route 2, Box 85
Supply, N.C. 28462

Cape Hatteras Anglers Club
P.O. Box 145
Buxton, N.C. 27920

Charlotte Offshore Sportfishing
   Club
5518 Spearmint Drive
Charlotte, N.C. 28212

New Hanover Fishing Club
P.O. Box 3512
Wilmington, N.C. 28406

North Carolina Beach Buggy
   Assocation
P.O. Box 969
Nags Head, N.C. 27959

Cape Lookout Mobile Fishermen
Star Route
Atlantic, N.C. 28511

Piedmont Offshore Club
P.O. Box 2768
High Point, N.C. 27621

Winston-Salem Sportfishing Club
P.O. Box 4212
Winston-Salem, N.C. 27115

Carolina Croaker & Marlin Club
P.O. Box 1172
Greenville, N.C. 27858

Charleston Shark Club
5465 Chisolm Road
Johns Island, S.C., 29445

Columbia Offshore Fishing
   Assocation
1331 Wellington Drive
Columbia, S.C. 29204

Florence Blue Water Fishing
   Club
187 Warley Street
Florence, S.C. 29502

Sea Island Sportfishing Society
P.O. Box 324
Isle of Palms, S.C. 29451

Saltwater Sports Club
P.O. Box 12852
Charleston, S.C. 29412

Edisto Beach Sportfishing Club
P.O. Box 18
Walterboro, S.C. 29488

South Carolina Saltwater
   Sportfishing Association
P.O. Box 2986
Charleston, S.C. 29403

Hilton Head Fishing Club
P.O. Box 2196
Hilton Head, S.C. 29925

Georgetown Sportfishing
   Association
P.O. Box 1704
Georgetown, S.C. 29440

Grand Strand Sportfishing
   Association
P.O. Box 3327
Myrtle Beach, S.C. 29578

FREE INFORMATION

South Carolina Sea Grant
221 Fort Johnson Road
Charleston, S.C. 29412

North Carolina Sea Grant
105 1911 Building
North Carolina State University
Raleigh, N.C. 27650

North Carolina Division of
   Marine Fisheries
P.O. Box 769
Morehead City, N.C. 28557

South Carolina Wildlife and
   Marine Resources Department
P.O. Box 12559
Charleston, S.C. 29412

South Atlantic Fishery
   Management Council
1 Southpark Circle, Suite 306
Charleston, S.C. 29407

OTHER SOURCES OF INFORMATION

(Your Senators)
United States Senate
Washington, D.C. 20505

(Your Representatives)
United States House of
   Representatives
Washington, D.C. 20515

National Coalition for Marine
   Conservation
P.O. Box 23298
Savannah, Ga. 31403

Sport Fishing Institute
1010 Massachusetts Avenue NW,
   Suite 100
Washington, D.C. 20001

International Game Fish
   Association
3000 E. Las Olas Boulevard
Fort Lauderdale, Fla. 33316

FISHING KNOTS

Courtesy of DuPont

Knots to Hold Terminal Tackle

Improved Clinch Knot

This is a good knot for making terminal-tackle connections and is best used for lines up to 20-pound test. It is a preferred knot by professional fishermen and angling authorities.

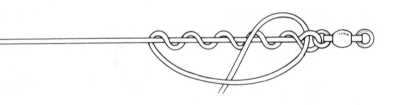

1. Pass line through eye of hook, swivel, or lure. Double back and make five turns around the standing line. Hold coils in place; thread end of line around first loop above the eye, then through big loop as shown.

2. Hold tag end and standing line while coils are pulled up. Take care that coils are in spiral, not lapping over each other. Slide tight against eye. Clip tag end.

Albright Special

This knot is used for tying a light line to a heavy monofilament leader or a wire leader.

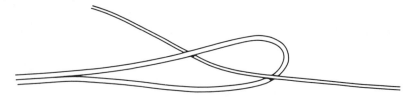

1. Double back a couple inches of the heavy line and insert about 10 inches of the light line through the loop in the heavy line.

2. Wrap the light line back over itself and over both strands of the heavy line. While doing this you are gripping the light line and both leader strands with thumb and finger of your left hand, and winding with your right.

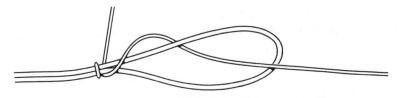

3. Make ten turns, then insert the end of the line back through the loop once more at the point of original entry.

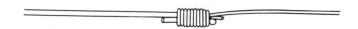

4. Pull gently on both ends of heavy line sliding knot toward loop. Remove slack by pulling on standing and tag ends of light line. Pull both standing lines as tight as possible and clip off excess from both tag ends.

Dropper Loop

This forms a loop in the middle of an otherwise unknotted line and to which a hook, sinker or fly can be attached.

1. Form a loop in the line.

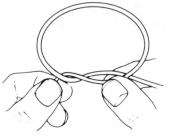

2. Pull one side of the loop down and begin taking turns with it around the standing line. Keep point where turns are made open so turns gather equally on each side.

3. After eight to ten turns, reach through center opening and pull remaining loop through. Keep finger in this loop so it will not spring back.

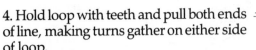
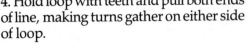

4. Hold loop with teeth and pull both ends of line, making turns gather on either side of loop.

5. Set knot by pulling lines as tightly as possible. Tightening coils will make loop stand out perpendicular to line. This is not a strong knot but it is useful for panfish and small saltwater species.

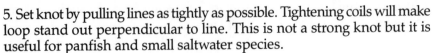

Knots to Form Double-Line Leaders

Bimini Twist
The Bimini Twist creates a long length of doubled line that is stronger than the single strand of the standing line. It is most often used in offshore trolling, but is applicable in light tackle trolling in both fresh and salt water.

1. Measure a little more than twice the footage you'll want for the double-line leader. Bring end back to standing line and hold together. Rotate end of loop 20 times, putting twists in it.

2. Spread loop to force twists together about 10 inches below tag end. Step both feet through loop and bring it up around knees so pressure can be placed on column of twists by spreading knees apart.

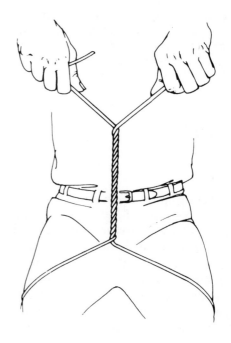

3. With twists forced tightly together, hold standing line in one hand with tension just slightly off the vertical position. With other hand, move tag end to position at right angle to twists. Keeping tension on loop with knees, gradually ease tension of tag end so it will roll over the column of twists, beginning just below the upper twist.

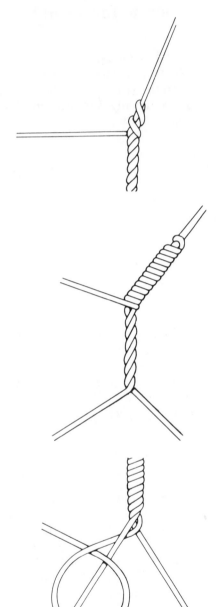

4. Spread legs apart slowly to maintain pressure on loop. Steer tag end into a tight spiral coil as it continues to roll over twisted line.

5. When spiral of tag end has rolled over column of twists, continue keeping knee pressure on loop and move hand which has held standing line down to grasp knot. Place finger in crotch of line where loop joins knot to prevent slippage of last turn. Take half-hitch with tag end around the nearest leg of loop and pull up tight.

6. With half-hitch holding knot, release knee pressure but keep loop stretched out tight. Using remaining tag end, take half-hitch around both legs of loop, but do not pull tight.

7. Make two more turns with the tag end around both legs of the loop, winding inside the bend of line formed by the loose half-hitch and toward the main knot. Pull tag end slowly, forcing the three loops to gather in a spiral.

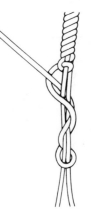

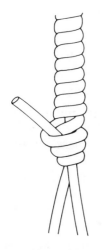

8. When loops are pulled up nearly against main knot, tighten to lock knot in place. Trim end about ¼ inch from knot.

These directions apply to tying double-line leaders of around 5 feet or less. For longer double-line sections, two people may be required to hold the line and make initial twists.

Spider Hitch

This is a fast, easy knot for creating a double-line leader. Under steady pressure it is equally strong but does not have the resilience of the Bimini Twist under sharp impact. It is not practical, however, with lines above 30-pound test.

1. Form a loop of the leader length desired. Near the point where it meets the standing line, twist a section into a small reverse loop.

2. Hold small loop between thumb and forefinger with thumb extended well above finger and loop standing out beyond end of thumb.

3. Wind double line around both thumb and loop, taking five turns. Pass remainder of large loop through the smaller one and pull to make five turns unwind off the thumb.

4. Pull turns around the base of the loop up tight and snip off tag end.

The Uni-Knot System

Here is a system that uses one basic knot for a variety of applications. Developed by Vic Dunaway, author of numerous books on fishing and editor of "Florida Sportsman" magazine, the Uni-Knot can be varied to meet virtually every knot tying need in either fresh or saltwater fishing.

Tying to Terminal Tackle

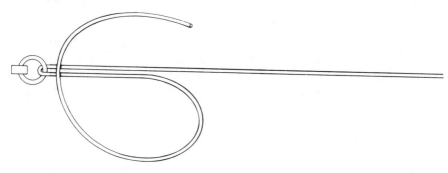

1. Run line through eye of hook, swivel or lure at least 6 inches and fold to make two parallel lines. Bring end of line back in a circle toward hook or lure.

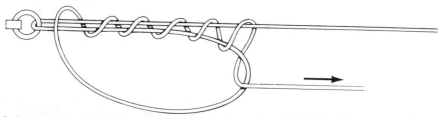

2. Make six turns with tag end around the double line and through the circle. Hold double line at point where it passes through eye and pull tag end to snug up turns.

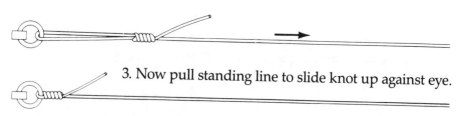

3. Now pull standing line to slide knot up against eye.

4. Continue pulling until knot is tight. Trim tag end flush with closest coil of knot. Uni-Knot will not slip.

Loop Connection

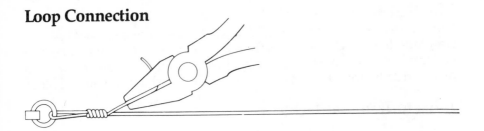

Tie same knot to point where turns are snugged up around standing line. Slide knot toward eye until loop size desired is reached. Pull tag end with pliers to maximum tightness. This gives lure or fly natural free movement in water. When fish is hooked, knot will slide tight against eye.

Joining Lines

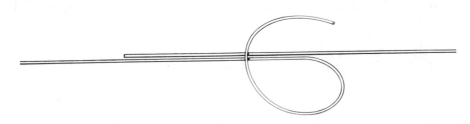

1. Overlap ends of two lines of about the same diameter for about 6 inches. With one end, form Uni-Knot circle, crossing the two lines about midway of overlapped distance.

2. Tie Uni-Knot around leader with doubled line. Use five turns and snug up.

3. Pull tag end to snug knot tight around line.

4. Pull knots together as tightly as possible and trim ends and loop.

5. Pull the two standing lines in opposite directions to slide knots together. Pull as tight as possible and snip ends close to nearest coil.

INDEX

192